L. WINIFRED BRYCE (left) appears here with one of her many Indian friends, Madame Vijayalakshmi Pandit (née Nehru), former Chairman of the United Nations General Assembly.

Dr. Bryce and her husband spent forty years in India as social workers and educators. She set up the school of social work in Indore and after "retirement" returned to help the school she loved to adjust to the standards of a new university.

Educated in Canada, Dr. Bryce received a Doctorate in Sociology at the University of Toronto. She is the author of seven books published both in English and Hindi. Her book *India at the Threshold* is well-known in America and England.

India

Land of Rivers

सत्यमेव जयते

BY L. WINIFRED BRYCE

The Child in the Midst
Comrades of the Road
Dhula the Bhil
India at the Threshold
Women's Folk Songs of Rajputana

India

Land of Rivers

L. Winifred Bryce

THOMAS NELSON & SONS

All photographs are from the Government of India except the following: Agricultural Missions Inc., pp. 97, 98, 101, 103, 104, 105, 124 (upper), 134, 140; L. Winifred Bryce, pp. 110, 113, 114, 115, 155, 174, 175, 200, 204, 205; Care, Inc., p. 206; Dr. D. F. Ebright, pp. 26 (upper left and right), 33, 138, 139, 186; Hugh Irwin, pp. 26 (lower), 27 (upper right), 30, 38, 112; Mrs. Van Itterson, pp. 94, 107, 127, 128; Methodist Missions, p. 108; Miller Services, Ltd., p. 196; Peace Corps, pp. 36, 111, 125 (lower); Royal Ontario Museum, University of Toronto, p. 27; Wide World Photos, Inc., pp. 74, 192. Permission is gratefully acknowledged. Map of India, p. 10, by Carmen DelBusto; diagram of rural village, p. 93, by N. M. Katary.

Library of Congress Catalog Card Number: 66-13840

Printed in the United States of America

Passage to India

Passage to India!
Cooling airs from Caucasus, far, soothing cradle of man,
The river Euphrates flowing, the past lit up again.

Lo soul, the retrospect brought forward,
The old, most populous, wealthiest of earth's lands,
The streams of the Indus and the Ganges and their many
  affluents, . . .
The tale of Alexander on his warlike marches suddenly dying,
On one side China and on the other side Persia and Arabia,
To the south the great seas and the Bay of Bengal,
The flowing literatures, tremendous epics, religions, castes,
Old occult Brahma interminably far back, the tender and junior
  Buddha,
Central and southern empires and all their belongings, possessors,
The wars of Tamerlane, the reign of Aurangzebe,
The traders, rulers, explorers, Moslems, Venetians, Byzantium,
  the Arabs, Portuguese,
The first travelers famous yet, Marco Polo, Batouta the Moor,
Doubts to be solv'd, the map incognita, blanks to be fill'd,
The foot of man unstay'd, the hands never at rest,
Thyself O soul that will not brook a challenge.

—WALT WHITMAN

India's National Anthem

India's national anthem, *Jana-gana-mana*, was composed by Rabindranath Tagore in 1911 and adopted as the national anthem in 1950. This is the poet's own translation of the song into English. (Note the mention of the mountains and rivers in the song.)

Thou art the ruler of the minds of all people,
dispenser of India's destiny.

Thy name rouses the hearts of the Punjab, Sind, Gujrat and Maratha, of the Dravid and Orissa and Bengal;

It echoes in the hills of the Vindhyas and Himalayas, mingles in the music of the Jumna and Ganges and is chanted by the waves of the Indian Sea.

They pray for thy blessings and sing thy praise.

The saving of all people is in thy hand, thou dispenser of India's destiny.

Victory, victory, victory to thee.

Foreword

I have much pleasure in writing a few lines to introduce Dr. L. Winifred Bryce's most interesting book. The author has lived in India, studied its people and its civilization through personal contact with rural and urban peoples of that old, but forever new land, which has been the home of the most ancient civilizations, dating back 5,000 years.

She starts her narrative from the hoary prehistoric times when the ancient Aryans of Central Asia started their arduous migrations in search of green land as fodder for their animals, some going towards the western lands of Greece and Rome and others moving to the southeast, crossing the great wall of the Himalayas, entered the subcontinent, where they settled down in groups in the valley of the sacred river of *Ganga*. She brings to you in her own fascinating way the story of the development of these gifted people from those hazy days to the present day.

During these thousands of years India, as well as the whole world, has lived through many epoch-making periods, the history of which is difficult to trace. But the distinguished author has taken full advantage of the scanty material available and has brought to light the great contribution to world civilization made by India in philosophy, science, religion, spirituality, and most of all, simple living and high thinking.

She has spoken about the arts of India—her architecture, statuary, painting, music—and has lucidly explained the variations that exist between the different schools which have developed their own effective styles during the centuries.

Towards the concluding part of the book, she has pressed into service the ancient system of imparting knowledge by the dialogue method. Two North American boys who are visiting India during the course of their university vacation are asking a hundred and one questions from an elderly village headman to understand the complicated social system of India on their visit of exploration to a newly developing village. This interesting dialogue gives glimpses of the work being done by the Government and the people in the hitherto sleeping villages as a result of which widespread awakening is taking place in this old country which is now on the march.

In short, this small book compresses in itself a fund of knowledge concerning India. It is easy reading, and has the charming fascination of a novel. It deserves to be listed among the high school and university textbooks on history, in the educational curricula and should be kept on the shelves of all libraries. It will not give to the reader complete knowledge of the country about which it is written, but it will awaken his interest and his desire to learn more. Mrs. Bryce has done a great service to the seekers of knowledge and I have much pleasure in recommending her book to those who want to know.

Rameshwari Nehru

Acknowledgments

An Indian friend, now a Canadian citizen, once humorously remarked that both he and I were "marginal people," neither belonging entirely to any one country or culture. I am grateful for my birth and mature years in Asia, and my education and later years in Canada, though sometimes I am not sure whether I am writing about India from the inside or the outside. To me India is one of the most wonderful countries in the world, not only because of her achievements, but because of her potential. She has my deep and respectful affection.

It has, therefore, been a great pleasure to have attempted to interpret India in a modest way. For obvious reasons much had to be omitted, and if any reader feels the loss I can only express my regret.

The pictures will, however, more than compensate for lack of words. Many friends and organizations have contributed and I thank them. Agencies of the Government of India (External Affairs, New Delhi; the High Commissioner for India, Ottawa; and the India Tourist Office, Toronto) were more than generous.

Useful suggestions have been made by several people who read the manuscript, and I thank them. My grandchildren, especially, were stern but helpful critics. I hasten to add that the faults which remain are indeed mine.

With appreciation for
his unfailing interest and understanding
and his sensitivity to India
I dedicate this book to
GORDON

L. Winifred Bryce

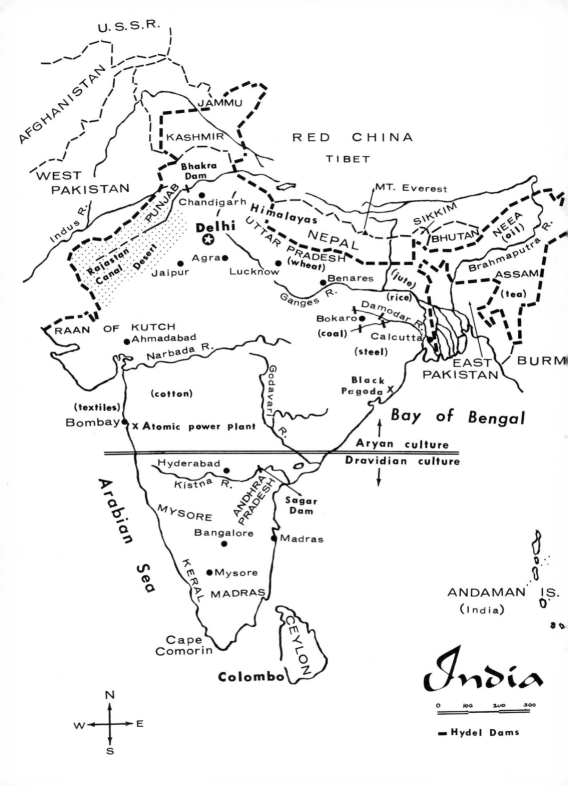

Contents

Shore temples at Mahabalipuram. These temples are not built but carved out of rock

Age cannot wither her, nor custom stale
Her infinite variety.

—SHAKESPEARE

Land of Rivers

India, with a population of well over 400 million people, is a country so vast and complex that a visitor often feels confused. The streets are crowded, and the passer-by may hear half-a-dozen languages. In some places public notices are posted in three scripts. Even the sense of time becomes baffled, for it is possible to pass in a few hours from the huts of tribal people who still use bows and arrows to a nearby city where great mills are working around the clock.

Even the name of the country varies. India has been called by many names, though that peculiarity is not hers alone. Some of the Indian postage stamps bear the words "Bharat India." The most widely known name, India, will be used in this book. It comes from one of the great rivers to the northwest, now shared with Pakistan, over which the Persians and the Greeks had to pass when they invaded India centuries ago. The name of the river was Sindhu, but the Greeks called it the Indus. Later the Muslim invaders called the area they governed Hindustan, which also comes from Indus. The term "Hindu" is reserved for followers of the religion known as Hinduism. Today the great population of varied races and creeds is known simply and proudly as Indians.

The Great Wall of India

The great wall of India is one of nature's triumphs. Stretching in a curve across the northern boundary of India is the most stupendous mountain range in the world. It is made up of a series of ranges such

13

as the Hindu Kush, the Karakoram, and the Great Himalaya, but the name "Himalaya" is often loosely and conveniently applied to the entire complex. It means the "abode of snow." The main Himalaya alone extends for 1,500 miles. Ninety-two peaks which exceed an altitude of 24,000 feet are in the Himalaya and the adjacent Karakoram range. The highest mountain in the world (29,028 feet), named Everest after the British engineer who first put it on a map, is in this range.

Astonishingly, there was a time when there were indeed no Himalayas; where they now stand was once a sea. Traces of marine life have been found in recent times on the mountain peaks. Eventually there was a moving together of the core of peninsular India and the core of the Siberian tableland; the earth crumpled and folded in what must have been one of the greatest earth movements on this planet. The rugged nature of the terrain that resulted is impossible to describe, but a suggestion can be given by noting that for part of its course the Indus flows through a great gorge with sides up to 1,500 feet high.

Alluvial plains lie at the foot of the lower hills which lead up to the higher mountains. These plains are made of the silt that is carried down when the tempestuous flow of waters takes place after the spring thaw. The snows on the heights, often referred to as the "eternal snows," are of course unaffected.

The Vindhyan Heartland

If the Himalayas are among the youngest mountains of the world, quite the opposite is the case with the Vindhyan Hills in the center of India. They constitute the core of peninsular India and are of extremely ancient origin. The passing of many years and erosion by wind and rain have reduced their once towering peaks, but a striking feature which may still be seen is the escarpment which faces south and east at heights of 1,500 to 1,800 feet. This resembles the Niagara peninsular escarpment which is familiar to travelers in southern Ontario.

South of the Vindhyas is an extensive plateau which is known as the Deccan (southland). A line of hills runs down each side of southern India. These hills are known as the *ghats,* or steps, dropping to the

14

Perennial snow in the Himalayas

shore line of the Arabian Sea on the west and the Bay of Bengal on the east. Most of the rivers in the south run into the Bay of Bengal because this part of India is tilted from west to east.

The Climate and Weather

The northern wall of mountains has had a considerable effect on the climate of India. We usually think of India as a tropical country, although actually only half of it lies to the south of the Tropic of Cancer. India is protected from the winds that blow across Central Asia, with the result that even the northern area is so sheltered that near-tropical conditions prevail.

The monsoon winds and rains of India have a character of their own because of the mountain barrier. Unlike monsoons elsewhere, the wind sweeps across the Arabian Sea bringing rain with it. It first "breaks" on the southwest coast, advances "up country" toward the northeast, is checked by the mountains, and eventually returns with somewhat diminished strength as the northeast monsoon.

The rainfall varies considerably. From the point of view of the farmer, it is said that in every five years there is one good monsoon, one bad monsoon, and three that are middling. That is why it is of the utmost importance to develop more reliable sources of water. Even in a single year there are marked differences between one part of India and another. The deserts of the northwest have little or no rain, and such as falls may be local. In Rajasthan there is a saying that rain may fall on one horn of a cow and not on the other. Fortunately, most of the country has what may be called a moderate rainfall of 45 inches, but the world record for abundance is held by the weather station at Cherrapunji in Assam where the average fall is 428 inches. The record there is said to be 905 inches, of which 500 fell in two months. A visitor to Cherrapunji came back with two stories about the rainfall. According to one story, a detachment of troops stationed there became so depressed by incessant rain that they poured water into the rain gauge to emphasize the situation. When even Cherrapunji recorded an unheard-of total, a checker was dispatched. The other told of the opposite method tried by a postmaster whose duty it was to record the rainfall. He ceased to send in reports, and when questioned about it, he replied that he was used to keeping rainfall records in inches, not feet.

India is generally thought of as a hot country, but there is more variability than might be expected as altitude is as important as lati-

Houseboats on a lake in Kashmir

tude for producing comfortable temperatures. It is possible to ski or skate in Simla in winter, and the schools which are situated in the hills have their long vacation in winter. The southern regions have a higher average temperature than the north, but at no season have comparable extremes. Temperatures of 115° to 120° F. are not uncommon in Punjab summers, but there is a correspondingly cold winter. Humidity is nil or almost so in the hot weather, excessive in the rains, and moderate in the cold weather. The well-known "hill stations" or resorts are patronized for about six months of the year and at 7,000 to 8,000 feet of altitude are very pleasant.

Generally speaking, India has three seasons in the year. The cold season occurs from November to February, and this is the ideal time for visitors from abroad. The hot weather lasts from March until the monsoon breaks in June. Then follow the rains which fall intermittently until the end of September, with October as a period of transition. There are occasional winter showers, but for the most part the weather is clear and predictable at that season—ideal picnic weather.

The Rivers

Besides the mountains the other important fact in India is her great rivers. As in some other countries they have played a significant part in her history. Alexander the Great, after a long and victorious campaign, halted on the banks of the Beas, one of the five rivers of the Punjab. It is part of the Indus Valley system in the northwest; other important rivers are the Ganges in the northeast, the Godavari of the southeast, and the Narbada, which is a natural boundary between north and south. "From the Indus to the Brahmaputra" describes the sweep of north India.

Rivers in India are sacred and are worshipped by Hindus as mothers and goddesses. Associated with them is a treasury of stories and rituals. The legend of Mother Ganges (*Ganga mata*) will illustrate this.

The river Ganges first emerged from the foot of the god Vishnu. After passing across the heavens as the Milky Way, she came down to earth in response to the prayers of a saint. In transit she passed through the long locks of the god Siva, who is said to have had seven

17

streams in his hair. Thus she came down to earth in the Himalayas, where the Ganges has its source, and flowed on to the thirsty plains.

On the banks of the Ganges is the city of Benares, the second oldest city in India, and much visited by travelers and pilgrims. At that place the bank of the river is lined with temples and with broad flights of steps on which sit ascetics in meditation. Pious Hindus bathe and pray in large numbers as the morning sun lights up the scene. Hindus feel that their salvation is assured if they can end their days by this river or if their ashes are carried away by its current. The ashes of many famous people, including Mohandas Gandhi and Jawaharlal Nehru, have been consigned to the Ganges.

The emphasis on legend and ritual is another way of saying how important the rivers are to people. Much progress has been made in harnessing the rivers to the service of man. Most of them are no longer used for transportation, but irrigation and power projects largely depend on rivers.

Harnessing the Rivers

The course of the monsoon and the currents of the rivers are problems with which India has struggled for centuries. Since the monsoons are variable, the rivers are variable too. In a dry season even a large river may almost disappear, while if the rains are abundant, flash floods may occur. Erosion has been almost unchecked, and rivers may change course drastically.

Remains have been found of ancient stone reservoirs, which indicate very fine engineering. One such reservoir had an embankment over one hundred feet wide at the base. We hear also of a famous engineer who was able to control the rivers "like a snake charmer his snakes."

Unfortunately, few of these former feats of engineering have survived, but a much humbler type has endured, built and kept in repair by the people of the countryside themselves by their own herculean labor. Whether it was a reservoir in which a number of villages shared, primarily for irrigation purposes, or smaller tanks for local and more varied use, the method was the same. It involved the construction of

18

Hirakud Dam on the Mahanadi River

an earthen embankment across a valley or depression to hold back the water until the time came for it to be released. Some modern reservoirs, which have been constructed on the old pattern and by the same expenditure of human effort, are capable of storing over 20,000 million cubic feet of water.

Wells also have been a widespread method of providing a steady water supply. Water for domestic use is drawn by women and conveyed to the village or the home in brass water pots on their heads. Men use bullocks in a variety of ways for the larger quantities required in irrigation.

19

Hunting is often done from the back of an elephant

During the last eighty years there has been a steady growth in government-organized irrigation works. From ten and a half million acres in 1878–79 the area annually irrigated rose to almost forty million acres in 1945. At that time India had the greatest irrigation system of any country in the world; it is still well in the lead.

After the coming of independence more modern methods were used, and the new dams and barrages are triumphs of engineering. They have become multipurpose projects and are economically sound. An experiment was tried with some of the projects to test the efficiency of an abundant supply of human labor versus machines. It was found that the benefit of increased employment for the rural population often outweighed a somewhat faster accomplishment by machines. The efficiency of the human labor rated high. This century tends to underestimate the great achievements of the past when human labor was the work unit.

Hydel

The developments which were part of the new planned economy in India have emphasized the multipurpose values of the hydro-electric (HYDEL) projects, which are completely changing the agricultural situation in India. To finance these enormous undertakings India has found help from friendly countries, both in the form of financial aid and in technical assistance. Some of this aid has been in the form of gifts and some in loans. In all cases India has matched the financial assistance, and her own planners and engineers have worked with the friends from abroad. The International Bank, the Colombo Plan, United States Technical Aid, the U.S.S.R., Western Germany, and Japan have been among those who have shared their resources and skills.

There are now twelve of these great projects either completed or well on the way. All of them are remarkable feats of engineering, and some are astonishing. The Hirakud Dam project is the world's longest dam and measures 15,748 feet. There are thirteen miles of dikes on both sides. The biggest multipurpose river valley scheme is known as the Bhakra Nangal project. The dam across the river is 740 feet high; there are about 652 miles of canals and over 2,000 miles of distributaries.

An often-quoted remark of Nehru is the reference he made to the new HYDEL projects as "the temples of modern India, worthy of becoming pilgrim centers." When we think of the food, the light, and the power that will be multiplied in this way, we can understand his enthusiasm. The projects are having a great effect on both industry and agriculture, and the lives of ordinary, hard-working men and women will be deeply changed. Flying over the plains of India by night, or journeying through the countryside after dark, travelers pass many villages without being aware of them as no lights may be seen. But on the periphery of a HYDEL project the little hamlets shine in the darkness as pools of twinkling lights. Here the comfort of light for the home and power for small industries has been achieved.

Young warriors from Assam in northeastern India

Where Did Indians Come From?

Periodically, Indian newspapers carry reports of a large group of nomads who have come over the borders of Kashmir and north India with their flocks and herds. They are usually assigned territory on which they can camp and even move about for better grazing.

In some such way the tribes who spoke an Aryan language came down into India from Central and Western Asia. The present-day nomads return to the highlands with the change of season, but the early Aryan tribesmen did not. They came in successive waves of migration, and probably the first waves consisted largely of men. More women came when the early adventurers had settled in the country. Kashmir where they entered is mountainous, but it has a wide and fertile valley known as the Vale of Kashmir. The adjacent part of India which consists largely of plains is known as the Punjab, which means "the Land of the Five Rivers."

Aryan Tribes on the Move

The Aryan tribes entered India about 2000 to 1500 B.C. They were part of a great movement of peoples in Central and Western Asia which drove some tribes south and east into India and others north and west into Europe. Perhaps, as in the case of present-day nomadic, pastoral people, the urge to move came through the need for grass and water; this would be of prime importance for people who lived as shepherds and herdsmen. A pastoral way of life makes a great demand on land, as a considerable area is needed for grazing. In regions where water and grass become scarce—especially water—there is often a fierce struggle for the right to use wells or for a share in the banks of rivers. A man might be killed for drawing water from a well that was not his own or for diverting his neighbor's watercourse. Water means life.

23

We must not, however, exclude the instinct for adventure and exploration which through the centuries has stimulated men. The stir of movement among these Aryan tribes must have been strong, for they went far. The resemblances between the people of Europe and India in feature and build is still apparent. There are linguistic relations also, for both northern and southern branches spoke an Aryan language which was the ancestor of Sanskrit in India and of Greek and Latin in Europe. We can still trace the common origin of a number of words in daily use, especially those referring to family relationships, such as *pitri* (Sanskrit), pater (Latin), father; *mata,* mater, mother; and other words such as *tara,* star; *agni,* ignite, fire; *khanda,* candy.

Aryan Religion and Poetry

The religion of these early Aryan tribesmen had two main features. First, like other people who have lived and moved freely out of doors, they were sensitive to the wonders of nature in both its kindly and its terrifying aspects. Like their cousins the Greeks, the Indo-Aryans personalized the forces of nature, such as the sun, moon, winds, fire, and worshipped them as divine beings to whom they referred as *devas,* the Shining Ones.

The other aspect of the early religion of the Aryans was quite unusual. Even before they entered India they had composed a number of hymns which were used in the worship of the gods. These hymns are said to be the finest group of poems ever composed by a people at such an early stage of their history. Even more remarkable is the fact that the hymns were not written down for a long time, indeed not until the Aryans had become settled in India, but they were memorized accurately and passed on with great care and reverence. The priests who had the responsibility for preserving the hymns and carrying on worship by sacrifices and offerings were highly respected. In the course of time four books were compiled which were known as the Vedas and are believed to contain some of the most ancient literature in the world. The oldest and in many ways the most remarkable part of the collection was known as the *Rig Veda.*

The Peacock Folk Dance in honor of Republic Day

Here is a translation of one of the poems.

Hymn to the Waters

("Ablution, bathing in holy lakes, rivers, the sea . . . plays a prominent part in Hindu rites and conduct. The following verses are always recited when water is thus used for purification.")

"O Waters! As you are the source of happiness, infuse strength into us, so that we have great and beautiful vision. That essence of yours which is most auspicious, let us share it here. O you who are like loving Mothers! Let us resort to you fully for that removal of evil, whereby you gratify us. Waters! You have verily created us."

As the Aryans spread down into the subcontinent of India they settled for the most part in the Ganges Plain which henceforth became identified with their culture and ethnic stock to a predominant extent. This area was frequently alluded to as Aryavarta.

It was not, however, a country which they could walk into and occupy, for there were already inhabitants with whom the Aryans had to come to terms. The people they encountered when they entered India were of three types: Dravidian, Negrito, and Proto-Australoid.

Dravidian Civilization

The Dravidians were established in India by the time the Aryans arrived, and they had developed a superior civilization of their own. Archaeological discoveries which took place about 1922–26 revealed that from about 3000 B.C. the Dravidian culture was centered in the cities of the Indus Valley. The two best known cities were Mohenjodaro and Harappa, and their discovery rolled back the known history of India by many centuries.

When the Indus Valley cities were inhabited and flourishing, they must have been among the most splendid cities in the world. City planning was excellent and astonishingly modern in many ways. The streets were laid out in city blocks and considering the type of traffic were quite wide—some thirty feet broad for a main street and fifteen for a secondary street. There was good sanitation, and even the two-storied houses had private drainage connecting with the main sewers. The houses were built of bricks much larger than those commonly used today; they measured about 15 by 6 inches and were about the thickness of a modern brick. The houses were apparently comfortable and fairly large. No place of worship has been found, but it has been suggested that the religious rituals of the citizens were concerned primarily with bathing and purification, and the city of Mohenjodaro had a large and important bathing pool in the center. Next to the pool are the remains of a spacious building which might have been the royal residence or perhaps the seat of government.

Not only were the builders of these cities good engineers, but they have also left a number of articles of artistic merit which indirectly give us a good deal of information about the life of that day. There are toys for children—miniature animals such as tigers, elephants, antelopes, and crocodiles. There is also a toy cart and an animal that moves his head. A number of pendants have been found which are probably

26

Ancient bronze statue of the god Siva with seven rivers in his hair

amulets. The pottery is beautiful both in shape and finish. A figurine of a dancing girl has become well known, and there are other small images and symbols of the god Siva who is still widely worshipped in India. Most interesting and important is the great variety of seals, for in those days contracts and other important documents were not often signed in writing as they would be today but were sealed with personal seals. They show engravings of many objects and animals, and by examining them we know that the climate was different from what it is now, as some of the animals represented are no longer found in that region. There are also a number of inscriptions, but unfortunately we do not yet know how to read the script. Some scholars have felt that they had come very near to understanding it, but their findings have not yet been accepted. If even one inscription could be found written in two languages, something could be discovered by comparison, just as the Rosetta stone of Egypt led to the deciphering of the hieroglyphics. It is possible that the language of the Indus Valley is related to

Belles of Serango in the Orissa jungles. Members of a pre-Dravidian tribe (left). Young Saora musician from a hill tribe (right)

Educated woman from the Bhil Tribe

28

*Tea picker of Darjeeling in north-
ern India. Many tea estates are in
the foothills of the Himalayas (left).
Bhil girl wearing the family's wealth
in jewelry (right)*

*Mother and child of Kashmir in the
snowy north*

29

Sumerian or a kindred language of the civilization of the Euphrates and Tigris rivers—another ancient culture based on rivers.

Why were those great and civilized cities of northwest India eventually deserted? This is a tantalizing question to which no answer can yet be given. We cannot even make a confident guess. It may have been due to war with invaders or to famine or to an epidemic or a change in the course of the Indus River caused by a change of climate. We can only hope that someday we shall find out. Probably further archaeological exploration will reveal how widespread was this early civilization. Explorations along the course of the Narbada River in western India have revealed a number of objects which have a marked resemblance to corresponding articles which were found in the Indus Valley. Obviously there was a connection, but whether travelers came overland or traveled by ship down the coast from the mouth of the Indus to the mouth of the Narbada and then went up the river for some distance, we do not know. The Narbada is still a river beloved by pilgrims.

As the Aryans established themselves in north India, the Dravidian people were pushed further south, leaving only pockets of their culture

Ancestral stones telling family history on graves of Bhil tribal people

and language. Eventually they passed over the Vindhya Hills and established themselves in the southern part of India, and there they still predominate. It was a long time before they built anything comparable with the Indus Valley cities, but they had other achievements. The metal which was developed in north India was copper, but in south India the more difficult metal, iron, was used at a surprisingly early date and began to take the place of the organized manufacture of stone implements. Another very early achievement of the Dravidians was the erection of stone monuments, megaliths or dolmens, which seems to be part of a pattern extending from Stonehenge in England, through parts of southern Europe and the Middle East, as far as south India. At a later period the Dravidians were the great temple builders, and their lofty and complex structures are still marked features of the cities of south India.

Negritoes, Proto-Australoids, and Other Ancient Peoples

There are Indians more ancient than even the undated Dravidians. We cannot guess at the dates of the earliest inhabitants, and archaeological research is very incomplete, but we have two sources of information: one is the effect they have had in various ways on those who came later, and the other is the amazing fact that there are still small groups or pockets of these aboriginal inhabitants leading their ancient mode of life in remote places in the hills or jungles. They belong to two distinct groups. The oldest are known as the Negritoes, as they have certain Negro-like characteristics. They are a small, dark people, forest dwellers, food gatherers rather than herdsmen or cultivators, and related to similar groups which are found on the periphery of southern Asia, in the Philippines, in Malaya, and, in their purest form in the Andaman Islands in the Bay of Bengal.

An illustration of the way in which a culture trait can be passed from one group to another in the course of many years is found in the respect these Negrito groups have for the *pipal,* a species of fig tree. This tree exudes a milky sap when a twig or even a leaf is broken off and is therefore regarded as a symbol of fertility, both human and animal. The veneration of the pipal tree was taken over by the Dravidians from their more primitive neighbors, and the pipal is now worshipped all over India by women who desire children. Often a little cradle or some baby clothes are hung on the tree as an offering, and if the prayer is granted, the woman does not forget to return with a thanks offering of a small coin or two or some food.

The Negritoes are believed to be the oldest people in India, but another ancient people came between the Negritoes and the Dravidians. They are commonly known as proto-Australoids, because they are apparently kin to the aboriginal people of Australia. At one time there was a shelf of land which made Asia and Australia more accessible to one another than they are today, and it is possible that the original people of Australia went there from India. They are short and have long heads with flattish noses, wavy or curly hair, and their color varies from dark to medium brown. Although they are found chiefly in south India, they are as a matter of fact quite widely dispersed and extend from the Veddas of Ceylon to the Mundas of east central India. We see individuals of this type scattered through the population almost all over India.

On the eastern side of India are people who are somewhat Mongoloid in appearance and thus similar to the people of Nepal and Tibet and other people in the lands on the eastern border between India and China.

Also in parts of India, especially toward the northwest, is a type of person that is sometimes called Oriental. These people are distinguished by a combination of fair skin, black hair, and dark eyes.

Thus we see that four major stocks of mankind are represented in India: the Negroid, the Australoid, the Mongoloid, and the Caucasoid. They have all contributed their special gifts and strengths, both material and cultural, and in this way combined to form the Indian people —a people of rare quality.

Religious Beliefs

Even today there are differences in religious concepts between the Aryan-based and the Dravidian-based areas of the country, in spite of the lapse of time and the skill and persistence of the Brahmans, Hindu

Two Saor boys dressed in ceremonial costumes for a festival in the Orissa jungle

priests and scholars, in bringing as much as possible under what is known as the umbrella of Hinduism. Beginning with the widespread acceptance of the four elements in nature—earth, air, fire, and water—it is apparent that the Aryans emphasized the gods of the air and their worship by sacrificial fire. The Dravidians emphasized purity rituals based on bathing ceremonies. They also worshipped with appropriate rites the deities or forces of the earth, which were connected with fertility cults. Again, the deities of the Aryans were predominantly male and their social system patriarchial. The Dravidians worshipped chiefly female deities, especially in rural areas, and their social system was matriarchial in emphasis. Some of the religious practices of the Dravidians were probably taken over from the still older peoples whom they had largely displaced. Probably it was the older influences which led to the use of magic in connection with religious practices.

Opinion is divided, but some authorities believe that the earliest form of the caste system (explained in Chapter 6) was Dravidian. Further research may throw light on this theory.

The vast complex which is known as Hinduism gathers together all these varying practices and beliefs. It is impossible in the scope of this book to give a comprehensive account of this ancient system, but for convenience we may accept the division into Higher, or philosophical, Hinduism and Popular Hinduism.

There are various ways of listing and classifying Higher Hindu philosophical systems, but the recognition of six "schools" is convenient.

The most famous school is probably the one known as *Vendanta*, which claims that there is but one Reality in the universe which is the supreme impersonal entity. When a man realizes that he is part of IT, he is released from the bonds of personality and rebirth.

Sacrifice was of great importance to the Aryans. It became the center of a philosophical system known as *Karma Mimamsa.*

The *Nyaya* is really a manual of logic, a subject which was emphasized in early educational systems.

The philosophy of *Yoga* has been much discussed in the West, especially in recent years, and has some followers in Europe and North America. This system teaches the importance of physical and mental self-discipline. The term comes from Sanskrit and is allied to the English word "yoke" as signifying both discipline and union.

The *Sankya* system is atheistic and is in effect an early system of mathematics and, to some extent, of psychology. The present science of "new mathematics" was perhaps anticipated by this school of philosophers.

Another forecast of modern science is found in the *Vaseshika,* which bases its thinking on physical science. It classifies observed phenomena and actually attributes the origin of the world to atoms, incredible though it may seem.

In addition to these philosophical speculations, Hindus from ancient times to the present day have accepted the concept of the four stages of a man's life:

In the first period he is a student, a Brahmachari, and lives a life of chastity and discipline under his teacher.

In the second period the man becomes a householder, earns his living, and does his duty to his family and the community in which he lives.

In the third stage the man is permitted to retire and lead a quiet life. In olden times he became a hermit in the forest and sometimes his wife accompanied him.

In the final stage the man becomes a homeless monk. He leaves his family and friends and spends his last days as a wanderer, as completely detached as a man can be from the affairs of life.

So-called "Popular Hinduism" ignores the philosophers and practices a variety of rituals based on sacred books written in modern languages, not in the Sanskrit of the classics. Philosophy needs no shrines, but Popular Hinduism does, and both the village shrines and the great temples which are characteristically found in the south are the concrete expression of a person-centered devotion and ritual.

Hinduism is nothing if not accommodating, so it is not surprising that it outlines four ways to salvation, and a person may choose the one he finds most helpful or thinks is most important.

There is first the way of knowledge, *jnana marg,* which is the way of the intellectual.

Yoga is the way of discipline of the mind and body.

Karma is the way of works, the practical way, suited to the householder and the man of affairs.

Bhakti is the way of devotion, which gives scope to emotion in the service of the soul. Many hymns have been written in the modern Indian languages which state in glowing terms the adoration of the devotee for his favorite god.

Indian Languages

One cannot travel in India without being impressed by the number and importance of the Indian languages. The Dravidian languages of south India have no relation to Sanskrit the classical Aryan language, though some Sanskrit words have been borrowed. Over two hundred languages, apart from dialects, have been recognized in India, but now

35

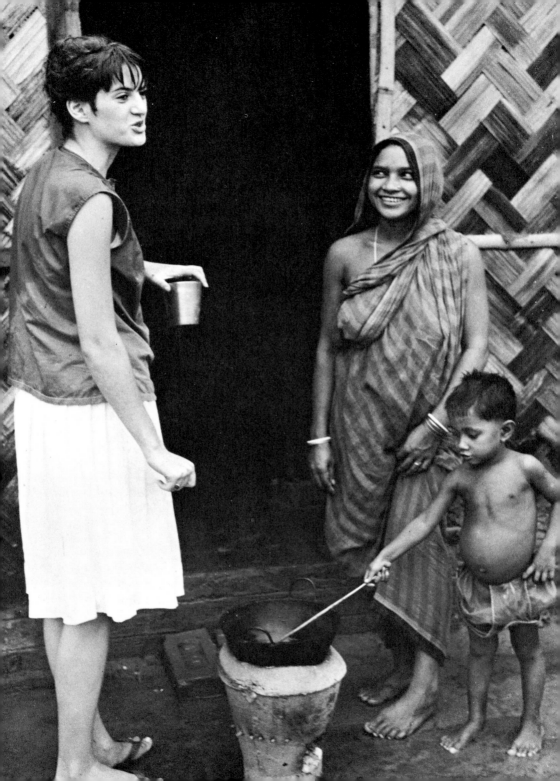

fourteen are recognized officially. Strong efforts are being made by the Hindi speaking people of the north to have their language adopted as the official language of the country, but there is considerable resistance to the idea, as the local or regional language is preferred for basic education, and English is still valued for higher education and international affairs. At present every child is likely to have to learn three languages at least. Fortunately, many Indians seem to have a gift for languages, and people who are unable to read any language are nevertheless often able to speak understandably in two or three languages besides their own. It is interesting to reflect that the linguistic problem which is one of those faced by India today has its roots in the confrontation of the Dravidian and Aryan civilizations some four thousand years ago.

A Note on Costume

A visitor to India soon learns to identify by various signs some of the variety of people he meets. One of the most useful guides is dress.

Travelers to India or those who meet Indians abroad unanimously praise the grace of the Indian woman's *sari*. The sari is a strip of cloth which a woman wears draped around her body in various ways. It is from 43 to 52 inches in width, and most saris now are from 5 to 7 yards in length, though only a few years ago some of them were 10 yards long to permit a certain type of draping.

The sari is draped around the waist with soft pleats hanging in front while the end of the sari is carried over the left shoulder and falls at the back. This is the way it is worn by the average educated woman. There are, however, variations. Some people prefer to throw the sari over the right shoulder instead of the left. Some draw the end over the head as a covering. Other women drape the sari around the legs separately to form a trouser effect which may be either loose or tight. It is said that one community of women who wear the sari in this way did so for ease in horseback riding. The sari draped in trouser effect re-

Peace Corps Volunteer cooking a meal with the help of a farm woman wearing a sari

quires extra yardage, and in the cloth rationing of World War II it was not so much used.

Not only the method of "tying" or adjusting the sari may be a matter of caste or ethnic preference but the width of the border or the material or the color may be socially prescribed. Two influences, however, have begun to modify these practices. The more frequent transfer of government or business employees from one part of the country to another has led to the borrowing of styles. Secondly, the great popularity of films has introduced the concept of fashion which was formerly unknown.

It is often assumed, even by Indians, that the sari as it is known to-

Bhil tribesman drying his dhoti after washing it in a nearby stream

day has been a classical garment, possibly influenced by the Greek colonists of northwest India. This pseudohistory has now been disproved by a careful study of sculpture and paintings. What was formerly called a sari was a waistcloth, similar to the Malay *sarong* (a word from the same root). The present-day sari developed from the head scarf or shawl and was not known until nearly the end of the eighteenth century.

In many parts of India the more ancient three-piece costume is still seen. It consists of a very full petticoat or skirt which may be six yards in circumference. With this is worn a bodice, usually small and tight, and over all the *orhni* or *dupatta,* which is a covering for the head. In the northern part of India both men and women wear *pyjamas* either tight or loose. With this is worn a tunic, and the women toss a scarf across the breast, and sometimes use it as head covering also. The pyjama is a daytime garment in India (from where it went to the West as night wear). It is accepted as a suitable and comfortable dress for girl athletes.

Men's clothing is now usually Western in style, especially in cities, but in rural areas one may still see the pyjama or the *dhoti.* The dhoti is not unlike a cotton sari, and it may be tied like a sarong or made into loose trousers. The turban or cap is still used, but chiefly by older men.

Details of dress are of social significance in most countries but perhaps especially so in India.

Leaping the Centuries

The thousand years from about 1000 B.C. to A.D. 1 have been called the great millennium. At the beginning of the period the Aryan tribes were still pushing their way south and east into the broad lands of the Ganges Plain. As they moved they settled in groups wherever they found an attractive or practical place. They continued to carry out their elaborate rituals and chant their ancient hymns, but they were entering one of the great creative periods of their history in which some of the finest literature of India was produced. Their minds roamed through more than one field of knowledge or speculation—mathematics, statecraft, and law. The name of Manu ranks with Hammurabi and Moses as one of the ancient lawgivers who laid the foundations of orderly government in the world.

By the seventh century B.C., therefore, the various Aryan tribes had more or less settled down and accommodated themselves to their new home and neighbors. The habits of tribal thought and practice still persisted to some extent, however, and tribes were grouped in small kingdoms. In one of these the ruler was the father of one of the most famous men in history—Gautama Buddha, a great reformer—whose message still appeals to men in the modern world.

Buddha and His Disciples

Gautama Buddha was born about 560 B.C. and died in 480. He was the son of a wealthy king whose capital lay one hundred miles north of the present city of Benares. Gautama's father wished to protect his son completely from any knowledge of the common ills and suffering

This Buddhist torana or gateway at Sanchi contains some of India's finest carvings

of humanity so he isolated Gautama as far as possible in a palace set in a park. The young prince was married to a beautiful bride, and they had a son. But Gautama's destiny lay elsewhere. At the age of twenty-nine by chance he saw four sights which changed his entire view of life. They were an old man, a sick man, a dead man, and a religious ascetic who sat lost in meditation and ignored the world. Gautama asked his charioteer the meaning of these things, and he was told that they were the common experiences of man. He felt impelled to explore the world himself, and one night slipped out of his home to search for the answer to the mystery of human suffering.

For the next six years Gautama tried one experience after another without satisfaction. At last when he was thirty-five, sitting in meditation under a tree, the "Great Enlightenment" came to him. Briefly his new view of life may be summed up in what he later called The Four Noble Truths:

> "All existence involves suffering
> Suffering is caused by unsatisfied desires
> Therefore desire must cease
> The Noble Eightfold Path outlines the principles of peaceful, ethical living that will lead to this sublimation."

Gautama spent the rest of his life preaching and teaching as he wandered across north India. He died at the age of eighty.

Since Buddhism is a creed that can be combined with other beliefs, it is difficult to say how many Buddhists there are in the world, but like Christianity and Islam it is a world faith as distinct from the religion of a people, or a national religion, such as Hinduism or Shinto. Buddhism is still followed by many millions of people in Asia. It almost died out of India, but there has been a revival in recent years, though not on a large scale. The most remarkable spread of Buddhism was in East and Southeast Asia, where art and other cultural patterns were markedly influenced. Buddhist temples are found in China, Korea, and Japan, and also in the countries now known as Thailand, Cambodia, Indonesia, and Vietnam. This expansion was assisted by the development of Indian trade, both by caravan and ship; thus a great cultural empire of Further India was established which brought education and the arts into many remote Asian areas.

An interesting offshoot of Buddhist culture is a collection of stories known as the Jataka, which became widely dispersed. In Greece some of them became part of the Aesop collection and emerged as stories about animals and human beings, often shrewd, sometimes humorous. They eventually became part of the traditional folklore of children of the Western countries.

The Great Epics

The most noteworthy literary achievement of the period was the growth and development of the great epics, which probably took form in the course of several hundred years. Although the name of Valmiki is linked with the *Ramayana* and that of Vyasa with the *Mahabharata,* there is little doubt that many minds and hands helped to shape them. Like the *Iliad* and *Odyssey* of the Greeks, the epics of India are enjoyed as good stories, though they may also be studied as history in its most picturesque form. Fortunately, there are several English translations.

The *Ramayana* is very much alive as stories from it are still told with zest, and the dramatic episodes may be seen on the stage in many villages. It is, briefly, the romantic story of Prince Rama and his beautiful wife, Sita, who followed him into exile. In the course of their wandering Sita was kidnapped and taken to Lanka (Ceylon). She was rescued by the combined efforts of her husband and Hanuman, the "king of the monkeys." Prince Rama was eventually restored to his kingdom.

The *Mahabharata* is much longer; in fact it is of such enormous length that it is seldom, if ever, printed in full. It is the source of many picturesque stories which gather around the long war between the Kauravas and their cousins the Pandavas. Besides the long narrative and the stirring incidents there are glimpses of the thinking of some three thousand years ago. We are startled by one such observation: "Space, which even the gods cannot measure, is full of blazing and self-luminous worlds."

The Great Stupa at Sanchi is a memorial shrine of the Buddha

The Bhagavad Gita

An important section of the *Mahabharata,* perhaps the most widely known and certainly the best loved Hindu scripture, is the *Bhagavad Gita,* "The Lord's Song." It continues to appear in new translations and editions. The *Gita* refers indirectly to philosophy but is mainly concerned with the lives of ordinary householders and their families.

The scene is set just before a great battle between the Kauravas and the Pandavas. Arjun, the hero of the *Gita,* is greatly troubled about this conflict between two hostile groups who are related to one another. His charioteer is no less than the god Krishna in disguise. Arjun confides his scruples and fears to him, and Krishna's advice is to do his duty. He is not responsible for all that is likely to happen, but he was born a warrior, and he must act accordingly. Krishna also speaks words of comfort and reassurance that the Divine Presence is at hand to help those who turn to Him. This summary, of course, gives no idea of the appeal this book makes to many persons who read it as their daily devotional scripture; as with other great books, the reader has to be attuned to what he reads.

Kingdom of Magadha

The rise of Buddhism and the great epics were but part of the ferment of ideas and the development in statecraft and the arts that took place in northern India. The climax was reached when the scattered small kingdoms became absorbed by the kingdom of the Mauryans, which was known as Magadha.

This kingdom was in touch with a number of foreign states or provinces, some of them at considerable distance. One of the countries which maintained an ambassador at the court of Magadha was Greece, and Megasthenes, the ambassador, has fortunately left a detailed description of what he saw in India during his appointment there (302 B.C.) in the reign of Chandragupta.

Megasthenes describes the capital city Pataliputra (now Patna) as splendidly laid out, a busy commercial center with wares from abroad as well as home products, inns for travelers, theaters and race courses for amusement, and also assembly halls for meetings of various kinds. A large army was maintained with the four divisions that were usual in antiquity: the elephant corps, the chariots, the cavalry, and the foot soldiers. There was an extensive system of roads from the capital to all parts of the kingdom, with a postal service. Megasthenes wrote also of the people of the country and particularly praised them for their remarkable honesty.

"No Indian," said he, "has ever been convicted of lying."

Chandragupta was succeeded by his son, who was also an able ruler, and he in turn was followed by Asoka, who was one of the world's great kings. Asoka reigned as Emperor of Magadha from 273 B.C. until his death in 232. His domains were the most extensive that had yet been known in India, but he began by plunging into war to extend his already ample boundaries. At the height of his success, however, Asoka met a Buddhist teacher who so influenced the young king that he began to think with horror of what he had done, and the peaceful development of law and order became his way of life.

Asoka published his edicts and laws by engraving them on rocks or on pillars set up in appropriate places. Several of these pillars have the lion capital which seems to have been a favorite design of Asoka and has now become the national emblem of India. The typical capital has four lions, standing back to back, on a platform or abacus. Below them is a band, or frieze, on which are sculptured the figures of a lion, a bull, a galloping horse, and an elephant, separated by wheels (*chakra*). Below that again is a bell-shaped lotus and then the shaft of the pillar. Obviously it would be impossible to show all sides of the pillar at once, so in the national emblem we see three lions, and beneath them a bull and a horse with a wheel between. The words inscribed below the emblem are from an ancient scripture, written in Sanskrit. The words are *Satyameva jayate,* meaning "Truth alone triumphs."

The wheel which is on the national emblem is also in the center of the national flag. Perhaps no modern government has adopted so ancient a symbol, but it is quite characteristic of India that she passes easily back and forth through the centuries. The wheel is, of course, full of symbolic meaning: primarily it is the Wheel of the Law, and by Law is meant both natural and moral Law.

To the end of his life Asoka was a devout Buddhist, and his missionary zeal led him to send messages of peace and piety to neighboring nations. Two of his sayings which have come down to us are:

"The reverberations of the war-drums became the reverberations of the drum of the Law."

"The conquest of the Law is also a conquest full of delight."

The Great Wheel of Konarak was carved about A.D. 1240

The yellow robe of the Buddhist monk has been familiar in Southeast Asia from the time of Asoka until the present day. Historians say that in the depth of his wisdom and the outreach of his influence the forty-year reign of Asoka is without parallel.

Kushan Invasion

The Mauryan Empire was followed by one of India's periodical dark ages which were characterized by fragmentation and general disorder. Once the firm control of the Mauryans had been relaxed, an astonishing variety of tribes began once more to pour through the gateway of India, the northwest passes. Some were transient, but others settled in India and made their contribution to the richness of Indian civilization.

The most important of the new invaders were the Kushans, under their king Kanishka. The chronology of this period is somewhat uncertain, but he probably ruled from A.D. 120 to 162 from his capital city of Peshawar. This choice of a capital in the northern part of his domains was due to the fact that the Kushans, like all Central Asian people, disliked the heat and spent their summers in the cooler climate of the northern highlands. Kanishka's state included not only northwest India but Afghanistan and adjacent areas.

By coins which were struck in that period, as well as by some sculpture, we know that the invaders were big, bearded men who wore padded coats and big boots. Their features were more Caucasian than Mongolian.

King Kanishka was a man of broad statesmanship, and he maintained good diplomatic relations with other countries, especially with the Romans; the eastern boundary of their empire at that time was less than six hundred miles from the Kushan kingdom. There was a brisk export trade from India in silk, spices, medicinal herbs, and other things. In that era the West had few goods which India desired, so the Romans paid in gold "aureus" coins which were valued as currency and a means of exchange throughout the East.

Like King Asoka, Kanishka was deeply influenced by the Buddhist faith, but he was wider in his sympathies and interests. Buddhism itself had developed along different lines from the Buddhism of Asoka's day. For instance, partly through the influence of Greek culture brought to India by Alexander the Great and other Greeks, for the first time images of Gautama Buddha were made, often of high artistic quality. This new form of Buddhism was carried to the east by the trade routes. Members of other religions were also recognized, including Christians who had entered India early in the Christian era and had become established.

With the death of Kanishka there came to an end a great period in the development of arts, culture, religion, and government. Once more the country entered a time of confusion. However, as always in India, the great majority of the people went about their accustomed tasks, most of them concerned with the production of food; to them the seasonal rains mattered very much more than who was in power. One of the coins of that period reminds us of this: instead of a monarch's head it shows the camel of Central Asia and the Indian bull. We have also a little plowing song with the same apt reminder; it is very similar to the plowing songs of today:

> "Bitter blue sky with no fleck of a cloud!
>   Ho! brother-ox drive the plow deep.
> Sky dappled grey like the partridge's breast!
>   Ho! brother-ox drive the plow straight.
> Merry drops slanting from East to West!
>   Oh! brother-ox drive home the wain.
> The gods give poor folk rain."

The Gupta Period

The next leap through the centuries brings us to the last of the great Hindu empires, which is known as the dynasty of the Great Guptas.

In the fourth century A.D. a new day dawned with the rise of Chandragupta, a bold adventurer, whose marriage to Kumari Devi, a princess of an ancient line, opened the path to the throne. After a short reign he died in A.D. 330, but he was succeeded by his son who ruled long

49

and well. Chandragupta's grandson, generally known by his title, Vikramaditya, the "Sun of Valor," succeeded to the throne in A.D. 380 and reigned for thirty-five years. Every now and then certain men in history seize upon popular imagination and attain immortality in the memories and even the affections of their people. Vikramaditya is still in his country the ideal story-book prince.

The Gupta and subsequent periods introduce us to one of the most surprising and interesting forms of international relations in the visits of several Chinese pilgrims, intrepid travelers, who faced the hazards of the long journey from their country to India, whether they came by land or sea. They had immense veneration for India as the land of the Buddha, and they wished to visit places connected with his life. They also had deep respect for the learning of India and came both to study and to take back to China important manuscripts. The Indians of that period were not much interested in history. Not until some centuries later did they write much about the significant events of their times, but the Chinese were good historians. They kept excellent records and published them when they returned to their own country. Many of these records have now been translated into English, and we can read the fresh, detailed accounts of the pilgrims who had almost photographic memories and unusual descriptive powers. Let us look at this era through the eyes of one of the most famous of these pilgrims.

A Monk-Historian

Hiuen-Tsang was born the youngest of four brothers in A.D. 603 in Honan, a northern province of China. One of these brothers was a Buddhist monk, and Hiuen-Tsang joined his brother's community at the age of thirteen. The next few years show a pattern similar to that followed by many students and other people in China in the twentieth century. Political troubles caused Hiuen-Tsang and one of his brothers to cross China to the western province of Sz'chuen and to take refuge in the capital city of Shing-tu (Chengtu).

Dilwara Temple, a Jain sanctuary at Mount Abu

51

At the age of twenty Hiuen-Tsang became a fully ordained *Bhiksu* (monk) and began to travel in search of more learning. When he was twenty-six he decided to go further afield, indeed to "go West," by which he meant to India. He received little encouragement from his friends, but some merchants from Tibet helped him with his plans, and eventually, after a journey of many months by an overland route he reached India. There he remained for fifteen years. He combined the life of a student with travels here and there, but above all he collected precious things to take back to China with him. His trophies included a number of relics, 6 images of Buddha, 120 copies of sacred books, 520 bundles of other writings; all these treasures were transported by twenty-two horses.

Concerning his impressions of India, Hiuen-Tsang writes with both observation and appreciation:

> "The towns and villages have inner gates; the walls are wide and high; the streets and lanes are tortuous, and the roads winding. The thoroughfares are dirty and the shops are arranged on both sides of the road with appropriate signs. Certain occupations have their abodes outside the city. In coming and going these persons are bound to keep to the left side of the road till they arrive at their homes. Their houses are surrounded by low walls and form the suburbs. . . . The monasteries are constructed with extraordinary skill. The doors, windows and the low walls are painted profusely."

Hiuen-Tsang speaks well of the common people and their cleanliness. He then continues, "Although they are naturally light-minded, yet they are upright and honorable. . . . They are faithful to their oaths and promises."

Public financing was done according to an interesting system.

> "The crown lands are divided into four parts. Profits from the first part are used for carrying on the affairs of state; the second, for paying the ministers and officers of the crown; the third, for rewarding men of genius; the fourth for giving alms to religious communities. In this way the taxes of the people are light and the services required of them are moderate."

The currency consisted of gold and silver coins, some of which have been preserved. Cowrie shells were used instead of coppers, and pearls were also used for currency.

Hiuen must have enjoyed his life as a scholar at the University of Nalanda in northeast India, for he seems to write with affection about the beauty of the campus. He says there were both open courts and secluded gardens; splendid trees cast a grateful shade which was enjoyed by those wishing to meditate; cool fountains of water gurgled delightfully in the hot season. A thousand inmates dwelt in six large blocks of buildings, four stories high, looking out on large courts.

In spite of the attractions of Nalanda, Hiuen-Tsang's heart turned with longing to his homeland, and packing up his treasures, he once more braved the dangers and difficulties of the road. He spent nearly twenty years happily editing the manuscripts he had brought from India and compiling his memoirs.

He left one great friend in India, Harsha the King. Harsha was undoubtedly Hiuen-Tsang's hero. "His skill in literature was profound," he writes. "His hands never hurt a living thing."

Soldier, administrator, poet, and dramatist, and deeply reverent in matters of religion, Harsha was the last outstanding Hindu king before the great change came to India.

The East bowed low before the blast
In patient, deep disdain;
She saw the legions thunder past
And plunged in thought again.
                    —MATTHEW ARNOLD

Delhi and the Grand Moguls

Tourists to India are often surprised to find that there are two Delhis, though it is difficult to find any open space between them as the land is all occupied. Old Delhi is centuries old, whereas New Delhi was built only in this century when it was proclaimed the capital of India on the occasion of the visit of King George V and Queen Mary. Most of the crowding is in Old Delhi; New Delhi is spacious. Wide vistas set off the many modern buildings, such as the House of the People (Parliament), the Secretariat, and the President's House. But the very spaciousness which is so enjoyable adds to the difficulty of moving about in the sprawling city. Aside from private cars there are many other kinds of transportation—the overcrowded public bus service, taxis, motorcycle rickshaws which rush about with considerable noise and fuss, and above all, thousands of bicycles which either weave in and out of the traffic or dash along the special paths provided for them in the main thoroughfares. Life is not easy for a pedestrian in Delhi!

Two college students threaded their way through the busy streets of New Delhi. For months Ted, a Canadian, and Jim, from the United States had been planning their visit to India. Delhi was high on the list of places they must see. All tourists, they were told, visited Delhi. Many tourists, however, spend only two or three days there and feel

A modern temple constructed of wood at New Delhi

55

quite overwhelmed by all there is to see, of both historical and contemporary interest.

Fortunately, the boys had introductions to some people in Delhi. There are several large modern hotels there, but Ted and Jim preferred to accept cordial invitations to stay with friends—or friends of friends—in a leisurely way. These visits gave them insights and opportunities that were invaluable. Since many people live under crowded conditions in Delhi with its population of over 2,500,000, Ted and Jim did not extend their visit indefinitely with any one family. They visited several homes in turn, and then took a room in a youth hostel where they met young men from all over India who were working in Delhi in government offices or commercial firms.

Now Ted and Jim were going to stay with Ahmed Shah, who was a teacher in one of Delhi's numerous high schools. He had met Jim's father while he was studying abroad and found that they shared an interest in history, the subject Ahmed Shah was now teaching. It was not surprising that Ahmed Shah soon impressed upon his young guests his belief that no one could possibly appreciate Delhi without knowing the history of the old city.

"As a matter of fact," said Ahmed Shah, "there have been seven Delhis. When the capital was moved from Calcutta and the proclamation was made at the Delhi Durbar of 1911, an old saying was revived that there would be seven Delhis and no more, and it was expected that the eighth Delhi would not last. Fortunately, it is still here," said Ahmed Shah with a smile, "and it is one of the finest capital cities in the world."

The new city is situated on a wide plain and also on the slopes of a low range of hills, usually referred to as the Ridge. New Delhi was planned by some of the leading architects and engineers of the world, and they had the advantage of starting with a free hand.

"Where are the old Delhis?" asked Ted.

"Scattered over the surrounding plain," was the reply. "Some of them are side by side and some are built one upon another. The first name of the city was Indraprastha; later it was changed to Dilli and then to Delhi. At any time of the year Delhi is beautiful, but perhaps most of all when the flowering trees, such as the blue jacaranda or the poinciana with its flaming blossoms, are at their best, or when the famous Delhi gardens are blazing with flowers in the sunny winter weeks."

Although Delhi is older than the Muslim period, it is most often associated with the thousand years in which the followers of Islam dominated the scene, and Ahmed Shah therefore said that Ted and Jim must begin with some knowledge of the religion known as Islam or Mohammedanism.

The Prophet

The prophet Mohammed, the founder of Islam, has an interesting story. He was born at Mecca in Arabia near the Red Sea in A.D. 570. Until the age of thirty-five he led the usual life of a trader of his day. Gradually he became dissatisfied with the moral deterioration of the

The Red Fort, Delhi. An historical site where large public meetings are still held

life around him, and thoughts of reform began to stir in his mind. His marriage to Khadijah, a wealthy woman of Mecca who had been his employer, gave him the leisure he needed to think out his convictions and make plans. At this time also he claimed to have visions and to receive guidance in his role as a prophet.

Twelve years later he incurred the wrath of those whom he had denounced, and fled from Mecca to Medina in A.D. 622. This flight known as the *Hejira* is considered a pivotal date in history by Muslims, and they date events from that year, A.H., just as Christians date from Anno Domini, A.D.

In Medina further developments took place in both Islamic creed and practice. The creed is short and simple:

"There is but one God and Mohammed is His Prophet."

His followers were required to pray five times a day, facing Mecca; to fast one month a year from sunrise to sunset, *Ramzan;* and to accept as their sacred book, the Koran, given to them by Mohammed. The word "Islam" means "surrender" or "submission," and Islam has been described as "The Religion of Submission to the World Potentate." The Brotherhood of all believers was also a cardinal belief.

Mohammed had no son, and on his death his followers were divided as to the succession. The Arabian Muslims held to the principle of electing their leader, whereas the Persians claimed that the leadership should be hereditary, through Ali, the son-in-law of Mohammed. The former sect is known as the *Sunnis* and the latter as the *Shias.* To this day they worship in different mosques and follow different customs. The feast of Mohorrum is celebrated as an occasion of rejoicing by the Sunnis and as a day of mourning by the Shias as it commemorates the death in battle of Husan and Hussain, the grandsons of the Prophet. To the world, Islam presents a monolithic front, but within its ranks traditions lead in different directions.

Together with Buddhism and Christianity, Islam claims to have a world message and accepts converts in many places. It is said there are more than 400 million adherents of this faith. Even in his time,

Mohammed saw his religion spread widely. It was a warlike faith, and the men who fought under the green banner of the Crescent believed that the shortest way to heaven was from the battlefield. They tolerated Christians and Jews to some extent, because they, with Muslims, honored the Old Testament scriptures ("the People of the Book"), but they considered all "idolaters" their lawful prey. This spirit has to be understood if we are to comprehend the force and drive with which the Muslims swept across north India.

Not all the Muslims who invaded India were of the same origin or culture. For easier understanding we may divide them into three groups: the early Turko-Afghans who were primarily raiders, the sultans of Delhi who restored a settled government, and the Moguls.

The Raiders

The earliest period lasted from the days of Mahmud of Ghazni, A.D. 997 to 1030, to the last of his line in the person of Muhammad Ghori, A.D. 1175 to 1206. These early invaders came simply and solely for loot. And what loot! Mahmud of Ghazni sacked north India no fewer than seventeen times. Toward the end of his life he was told of a warrior who had collected seven pounds of jewels, whereupon Mahmud gave devout thanks to God that he himself had collected more than one hundred pounds of gems. Muhammad Ghori's record is similar. These raiders were big, burly men with long noses and long curly beards who wore skin coats and carried long swords. They rode swift horses.

The Slave Kings—Sultans of Delhi

The sultans of Delhi restored order to the distracted country. They were led by the dynasty of the Slave Kings who through their shrewdness and the opportunity afforded by the brotherhood of Islam rose in power until they took the administration in their hands. The founder of the line was actually a slave in his early life. The Slave Kings ruled Delhi from 1206 to 1290, followed by three other dynasties: the Khiljis,

(1290 to 1320); the Tughlaks (1320 to 1388), and the Lodis (1450 to 1526). Their tombs, mosques, and fortifications, some of them well preserved, are scattered over the plains of Delhi for the historian's fascination.

Timur the Lame

In the gap between the Tughlaks and the Lodis appeared one of the most remarkable conquerors of world history, comparable only to Jenghiz Khan. His name was Tamerlane, or Timur the Lame.

Timur was a Turk whose hordes overran much of Central Asia and then marched into the Punjab in hope of plunder. A great organized battle between the Indian army and the invaders took place under the walls of Delhi in 1398. Timur with his 90,000 cavalry encountered the armored war elephants, which terrified most men who saw them for the first time much as the first sight of tanks startled and shocked the armies of World War I. One of Timur's weapons against the elephants was a device known as caltrops, four-spiked iron balls which had been designed to be thrown on the ground in front of cavalry horses to maim them. This weapon was used effectively against the elephants of India.

Timur did not, however, press his advantage but retired to his Central Asian stronghold. Just as the armies of Napoleon were defeated by the cold of "General Winter" in Russia, the summer heat of India more than once drove invaders back to the highlands of Central Asia. But the devastation left by Timur was unprecedented. Delhi was deserted. As Timur himself states it in his memoirs, "For two whole months not a bird moved a wing in the city."

After some time, however, the Lodi kings, the last of the sultans of Delhi, reoccupied the city and restored peace and order in their domains. The Lodis were followed in turn by more men from Central Asia but very different from those who had come before. These men were the Moguls.

Kutb Ninar, Delhi. A flight of 376 steps leads to the balconies and top of this tower

The "Grand Moguls" (1526 to 1707)

The name "Mogul" is confusing to the present-day reader. It is a form of the word "Mongol" which was, unfortunately, loosely used by the Portuguese in India. The Moguls did have a Mongolian strain, but their basic stock was from Central and Western Asia.

Babar the Tiger, the first of the Mogul emperors, took over his father's kingdom in Turkestan at the age of twelve. Through his father's line he was descended from Tamerlane and through his mother from Jenghiz Khan. No doubt the thought of his redoubtable ancestors influenced his dreams and ambitions. Babar must have read a passage from Tamerlane's autobiography in which his ancestor refers to his decision to conquer India. Tamerlane wrote:

> "I ordered one thousand swift-footed camels, one thousand swift-footed horses and one thousand swift-footed infantry to bring me word respecting the princes of India. I learnt that they were at variance one with another. . . . The conquest appeared to me easy, though my soldiers thought it dangerous.
>
> "Resolved to undertake it, and make myself master of the Indian Empire.
>
> "Did so."

It was, however, many years before Babar could seriously plan to take India; in fact he was forty-two before he began his march. He had first to establish himself in the turbulent, uneasy kingdom in Central Asia that he had inherited from his father. When he was twenty he lost a battle and took refuge in the hills where a shepherd sheltered him in his hut. Far in the distance lay the wide plain of India. As he gazed he listened to the tales of an old woman, ragged and frail, who told him stories of her youth, "when the earth trembled under Timur."

At last in 1525 he marched on India. Some of his troops were armed with matchlocks, a distinct advantage in fighting the Indian army which had few firearms. Babar had a man in his army who knew how to cast cannon and was able to build up a small but useful artillery, which was also an advantage.

62

There are some portraits of Babar at this time; they show a tall, muscular man, with the long, straight nose of his race. He had great personal strength and daring and has been thus described: "A man who swam every river he crossed for sheer joy in breasting a strong current; who lived in the saddle; who, if challenged, would snatch up a comrade in either arm and run around the battlements of a fort, in laughing derision."

Now that India had been conquered, Babar made his home in Agra, about 125 miles from Delhi. There his greatest pleasure was in the gardens where he collected flowers he had known and appreciated even during the wildest of his campaigns.

Warrior though he was, he had an affectionate family life. He especially adored his daughter, Gulbadan. Once after she had been absent from home for a long time, word was brought to Babar that her caravan was six miles away from the city. Without waiting for horse or even shoes, for he was wearing only light slippers, Babar leaped to his feet and ran to meet her, then walked beside her palanquin to bring her home.

Hamayun

Hamayun, the son of Babar, had a comparatively uneventful reign. His tomb is still to be seen in the environs of Delhi. His chief claim to fame is that he was the father of Akbar the Great, who was not only the greatest of the Moguls but one of the greatest kings in history.

Akbar the Great (1556 to 1605)

Akbar was undoubtedly an exceptional man. He was a contemporary of another strong personality, Queen Elizabeth I of England. It seems a pity that Akbar and Elizabeth never met.

Like his grandfather, Babar, Akbar came to his inheritance when he was very young: he was only thirteen. It took seven years for him to set his kingdom in order and be free to govern as he wished. He was a man around whom legends gathered, and few of his contem-

poraries could have understood him. He has been called the "Prince of Dreamers," but he was also a realistic man of action.

Unlike most of the other Moguls who have left vivid and picturesque memoirs, Akbar was illiterate; we are told that he could barely sign his name. He had, however, a liking for the company of men of various gifts: scientists, philosophers, artists, theologians. He enjoyed keen debates and had a retentive memory for what he heard. He had a strong strain of mysticism, but it was well balanced by his love of sport and feats of physical courage.

Visitors to Delhi or Agra usually travel about twenty-three miles out of Delhi to Fatehpur-Sikri, which is Akbar's city of Fatehpur built near the old village of Sikri. Fatehpur is a city of great beauty, built of red sandstone and white marble in noble designs. The king built it to honor a Muslim saint whose sanctity, he believed, was responsible for Akbar's good fortune in having three sons. Why the city was abandoned a few years later is not known. One explanation is that the water supply was inadequate. Another is that the saint tired of having his quiet life interrupted and bade the King and court withdraw. No one now lives in Fatehpur, though many visit it. From the great gateway of the city, said to be the highest in the world, the visitor can still see the little mud-walled village of Sikri that was there before the city was built and is still lived in.

By his thirty-fourth year Akbar had consolidated his empire and held the whole of north India from the Himalayas to the Vindhyas and from the Indus to the mouth of the Ganges. Henceforth he devoted himself to the arts of government, for his ideal was to make India a land of unity and mutual tolerance. To conquer an empire was one thing; to hold it for his descendants was another. The pen proved to be at least as mighty as the sword, and Akbar employed clever Hindus as secretaries and administrators. He also succeeded in making friends with some of the proud Rajput chiefs. He married a Hindu and a Christian and built a house for each one when he was building Fatehpur. Unlike others of his line he chose his friends wisely. The most famous character at the court and one about whom many stories are still told was Rajah Birbal, the court minstrel and jester, whose quaint humor and shrewd observations are still remembered. Many of Akbar's reforms lasted until recent times, and some are still part of the fabric of Indian administration.

Unfortunately, Akbar's sons did not match him in either strength or wisdom, and the Mogul tradition slowly waned in their reigns though outwardly the traditional pomp and splendor were maintained. Strangely, in the next two reigns the strongest characters were women.

Jahangir (1605 to 1627)

Jahangir, the son of Akbar, was first known as Prince Salim but took the title of Conqueror of the World, Jahangir, upon his succession. At the same time he conferred the title of Light of the World, Nur Jahan, on his wife.

Nur Jahan was born in the desert of refugee parents. Since they felt that the babe would be an encumbrance to them in their flight, she was laid in a shady spot near a desert shrub and abandoned. A merchant traveling that way saw the child and took her for his own. Eventually, in Agra, Nur Jahan's parents were reunited with their daughter, and her father was given a place of honor and responsibility at the court with the title of Itmad-ud-dowlah. When he died, his daughter erected over his tomb one of the loveliest buildings in Agra on the bank of the Jumna River. It is beautifully proportioned, and the lacelike panels of pierced marble are of the finest workmanship.

Nur Jahan not only was a woman of great beauty but was renowned for her courage and spirit. She was an accomplished horsewoman and intrepid hunter, and on one occasion she shot four tigers. She also had a keen mind and a fund of practical good sense. Unfortunately, Jahangir weakened in mind and body as the years passed and would hardly have been able to govern without Nur Jahan's help. The royal decrees were eventually signed by both Jahangir and Nur Jahan, which was a remarkable concession to a woman in that period.

Shahjahan (1627 to 1657)

Nur Jahan contrived that her niece, who became known as Mumtaz Mahal, should marry Jahangir's heir, Shahjahan. This queen is known all over the world, as the Taj Mahal in Agra was erected in her honor. She did not have the varied gifts of Nur Jahan, but she was immortalized by her husband as a devoted wife and mother. Shahjahan was as strong a ruler as his father had been weak, and in his reign India was peaceful and prosperous.

The Taj Mahal which Shahjahan erected over the grave of Mumtaz attracts visitors from all over the world; no woman ever had such a tribute. The Taj was in process of building from 1632 to 1647. Twenty thousand workmen were constantly employed. It is said to have cost four and a half million pounds sterling, but the equivalent cost today would be comparable only to the sums lavished on space exploration.

Shahjahan's reign ended most unhappily. He was captured by his son Aurangzeb and confined to rooms in Agra Fort. From the Jasmine Tower he spent his days looking across the river at the loveliness of

The Taj Mahal in Agra. The tomb of Mumtaz Mahal is usually photographed from the reflecting pool; this picture was taken from the riverside

67

his masterpiece and the resting place of his queen, the Taj Mahal. He was constantly attended by his devoted daughter, until at last in 1666 he was released by death and buried beside his beloved Mumtaz Mahal.

Aurangzeb (1658 to 1707)

The last of the great Moguls is known as the man without a heart. Aurangzeb was not able to hold his domains intact, and his successors lacked the vigor and statesmanship of the earlier Moguls. Eventually the Marathas in the west, the Rajputs in the north, and the Sikhs in the Punjab revolted. Finally the last of the Moguls, who had a decadent court in Lucknow, was deposed in 1858 when the government of India was assumed by the British Crown.

Delicately carved marble screen in the Taj Mahal, Agra

Islam and India

The later Moguls passed into oblivion, but the earlier Moguls are remembered for their many enduring legacies both material and cultural.

Since Ted and Jim had now become familiar with the outline of the thousand years of Muslim raid and rule and had spent a number of days in exploring the historic sites, they revisited Ahmed Shah to talk over their impressions with him. Their friend explained that the advent of the Muslims in India was the first serious interruption of Indian culture. The previous invaders had either been assimilated or they were accommodated in the social system. The followers of Islam and Hinduism could not be said to have achieved assimilation, as was seen when the country was partitioned as part of the process of gaining independence.

"Partition" is an unhappy word in both India and Pakistan, but Ted and Jim felt that it was of such importance that they must try to understand it. This is how Ahmed Shah outlined the events of those days.

In 1947 when India was on the eve of independence, the struggle between Hindus and Muslims which flared up seemed likely to wreck the plans for self-rule. The situation was met by a mutual agreement between the Indian National Congress and the Muslim League that the country should be partitioned into two nations, India and Pakistan —the latter with two areas, West and East. Each nation should have territory that was dominantly Hindu (India) or Muslim (Pakistan). The religious issues involved in Partition may remind people in Western countries of the wars of religion in Europe or of the fact that one important motive for immigration to America was the principle of religious liberty.

Religious differences, however, were not only a matter of creed or worship; they involved political ideology. Undoubtedly, religion was the major factor in Partition, but it is more accurate to say, in the words of an Indian correspondent, "The war over Kashmir symbolizes the clash of powerful ideas prevalent in the subcontinent—between the medieval concept of a religious state (as elaborated in the Pakistani

Constitution) and the more modern but difficult venture of a secular nation (as embodied in the Indian Constitution)."

In addition to factors of religion and political philosophy, a third point to be considered is the combined pressure of economics and natural resources. West Pakistan's rivers rise in Indian territory, and it was some time before an understanding could be reached between the two countries regarding the control of the waters, with all that was implied for the productivity of Pakistan. West Pakistan also looks with desire on the forest wealth of Kashmir. West Pakistan has no such resources readily available.

When religion, politics, and economics form a complex, the situation becomes both difficult and serious. The separation of the territory which resulted in the establishment of two distinct countries was effected as a result of painful stress, but India is learning to combine different elements as other countries in the world have done. As the Indian correspondent expressed it, "The day the wishes of India's 50 million Muslims are ignored, the fabric of secular India will be in tatters."

As a matter of fact the Indian Muslims are taking their share in the administration of the country. While the President of India, Sir S. Radhakrishnan, is a distinguished Hindu philosopher, the Vice-President is the no less distinguished Muslim educator, Zakir Hussain. India's chief representative to the United Nations is also a Muslim, Education Minister Mohammed Chagla. Three members of the Cabinet and several ambassadors are also from the Muslim community of India.

"Surely there must have been ways in which the Muslims and the Hindus interacted favorably at times in the past," said Jim.

"I understand that Islam does not practice caste," said Ted. "Did that affect Hinduism at all?"

"Yes," said Ahmed Shah, "it did in two ways. Quite a number of lower-caste Hindus became converts to Islam. In this way, they believed, they would be set free from caste and gain a new self-respect. In the same way a large number of lower-caste Hindus have become Christians. Another result was that some Hindus whose thinking had

70

Stone lacework in the Amber Palace at Rajasthan. An outstanding example of Mogul architecture

been influenced by the Muslim practice of the brotherhood of all believers initiated reform movements. They claimed that in God's sight men are equal and that men can reach God by more than one path."

One of the most famous of these reformers was Kabir, a humble weaver who became a saint. His poems are still sung all over the country.

Ahmed who had a fine voice began to sing:

"Oh Servant, where dost thou seek Me? Lo, I am beside thee.
I am neither in temple nor in mosque: I am neither in Kaaba
nor Kailash.
Neither am I in rites and ceremonies, nor in Yoga or renun-
ciation.
Kabir says: O Sadhu! God is the breath of all breath."

After a brief silence Jim turned to another subject, "It seemed to me that in spite of a general resemblance there was a good deal of variety in Mogul architecture. The earlier buildings had great strength and were very plain, but much beauty and a wealth of detail were developed as time went on."

"You are right," said Ahmed, "and you have seen the two currents in Islamic culture. The men of the desert among whom Islam began stood for strength and an austere simplicity. Later came influences from Persia, and the Muslims there were true Persians; they loved gay, flowery patterns in decoration of buildings and in rugs and textiles. They had a lightness of spirit which you would not expect from the desert Arabs."

"What lovely gardens they had!" said Ted. "And some of the present-day gardens in Delhi follow the Mogul pattern, don't they?"

"Yes," said Ahmed, "I am glad you noticed that. One of the Delhi sultans is said to have laid out twelve hundred gardens in and near Delhi and to have restored thirty others. The pleasure in gardens was shared by the Moguls and the British, who also were great garden lovers."

"Didn't the Hindus have gardens too?"

"Not so much as the Moguls. When the Hindus wanted to draw near to nature they went into the hills or the forests, but the Muslims brought into their environment the plants and flowers they enjoyed, often with the expenditure of considerable effort and expense. This love of plants and flowers was reflected in their handicrafts, as you have probably noticed, and especially in their paintings. Of course,

Hindus had long practiced the art of painting, but the Moguls introduced new forms such as miniatures. Did you ever hear this quotation from Akbar? 'The Painter has quite unusual means of recognizing the Creator. In sketching from life he must come to feel that he cannot bestow personality upon his work, for personality is the gift of God.' "

One thing Ted and Jim had noticed with interest in many of the buildings they had visited was the use of fine penmanship, or calligraphy, as part of the decoration. Arabic or Persian script lends itself to this use. The ninety-nine Names of God or texts from the Koran are used in this way.

Delhi is full of interesting handicrafts of many kinds, and this is largely the result of the long tradition whereby skilled jewelers, weavers, and calligraphers were permanently employed by the royal households and the courts. Musicians and poets were similarly encouraged. Writing and reciting poetry were social arts and fortunately still survive.

Through the contact of Arabs with both Europe and India, much learning was carried from India to the West. As a result both Greek and Sanskrit books were translated into Arabic. Our so-called Arabic numerals originated in India as did the concepts of the zero and of the decimal. Astronomical and medical theories passed from land to land, sometimes through travelers, though scholars corresponded across what seem to us incredible distances.

Stories have a particularly happy knack of traveling as they are told and retold around the campfires where the caravans meet at night. In this way the collection known as the *Arabian Nights* came to Europe. It includes stories from India and several other countries. "The Horse of Brass" which Chaucer retold comes from this collection, and so does the even more popular tale "Sinbad the Sailor."

Just as Chinese culture was invigorated in earlier times by Buddhism from India, so Indian culture in turn was stimulated by Islamic culture and its contacts with the West. And as Buddhism flowed east from India, so did the tide of Islam move on to Southeast Asia. India is still the meeting place of cultures.

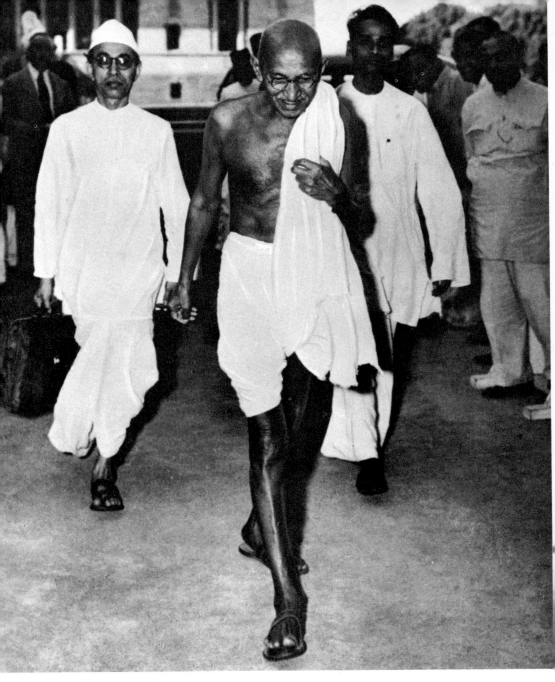

Mahatma Gandhi on his way to meet the British Cabinet Mission

74

India Achieves Nationhood

In the fifteenth century began a great era of exploration and adventure in many parts of the world. For the first time men sailed around the world—a feat as daring and exciting to the people of that age as space travel is to us.

In 1498 Vasco da Gama, an intrepid Portuguese navigator, astonished the people of the west coast of India by arriving with a fleet of three small ships in the harbor of Calicut. Heretofore all who entered India had come overland from the northwest, but now the sea route was open. Trading between Europe and India had been carried on for a long time, but it had been done by caravan. The rise of Muslim power had disrupted these trade routes, and there was urgent need of establishing new communications. The wealth of India was still a lure, though the appeal was different. No longer was it chiefly gold and gems, but textiles, medicinal herbs, and above all spices that were in demand—spices to lend variety to the dull food of the period and also to act as a preservative of meat.

It will be remembered that it was the quest for India that drove Columbus across the Atlantic. An Indian speaker once humorously reminded his American audience that they owed the discovery of *their* country to the search for *his*!

The search for "the gorgeous East" continued until Vasco da Gama anchored at Calicut, made overtures to the local ruler, and returned home with a cargo of spices and precious stones that was described as "priceless." He also took some of the fine cotton textiles that were available at Calicut and introduced them to Europe under the name of *calico*.

The Portuguese continued to explore the shores of India and went even further east. The most famous of their adventurers was Affonso de Albuquerque who was a farsighted and able man. He set up the

75

Monument marking the landing point of Vasco da Gama at Calicut in 1498

VASCO - DA - GAMA
LANDED
HERE
KAPPKaDAVU
IN THE YEAR
1498.

pattern of Portuguese expansion by establishing strategic posts, from Ormuz at the entrance of the Persian Gulf to Malacca in the East Indies. It is said that there have been few better geopoliticians than Albuquerque. Most important of all was his acquisition of the port of Goa, with splendid churches and public buildings, which became the capital of overseas Portugal; it was known as "Golden Goa." Goa remained a Portuguese possession until December, 1961, when India took it over.

The development of trade became a matter of widespread interest, and other European powers entered the competition. From the seventeenth century to the middle of the eighteenth, games of commerce and politics were played on a grand scale in three continents. The smaller powers were soon forced to drop out, though Denmark maintained two footholds in India until 1845. The chief competitors were the Dutch, the French, and the English. The main interest of the Dutch, however, lay east of India in the so-called Spice Islands, now known as Indonesia.

76

"The Game of French and English"

The French and English rivalry in India reflected the encounters of the two powers in Europe and America in the eighteenth century. Considering the difficulties of travel at that time and the length of the voyages, one is amazed to read how a man's career might begin in Europe, continue in America, and conclude in India.

One such example is Lord Charles Cornwallis. He was a brilliant soldier in the American War of Independence, but on the arrival of French troops to strengthen the American forces he was forced to capitulate at Yorktown. On his return to England, however, he found new challenges, and between 1786 and his death in 1805 he was appointed three times as governor-general and commander-in-chief in India.

Napoleon once referred to the English as "a nation of shopkeepers." It is one of the surprises of history that the British entered India as traders; the subsequent development of their interests and authority took place under the East India Company until the middle of the nineteenth century.

The first Englishman known to have visited India was a Jesuit priest in 1579. There were several adventurers after that, but only one man, Hawkins, stayed. The first ambassador to the Mogul Court was Sir Thomas Roe who came with credentials from James I in 1615. When he left four years later he had negotiated favorable terms for trade.

The East India Company, familiarly known as John Company, was established in 1600. Very different though it was from the Hudson's Bay Company (1670), both of them reflect the daring mood and the breadth of interests prevailing in England in that century. There has never been anything quite like those two companies which led men of the countinghouse and restless young men with an uncertain future into empire building through commerce.

Curiously, both companies used the word "factory" to mean not a place of manufacture but a trading station. The first factory of the East India Company was in Surat (1609) on the east coast, where the Dutch also had a factory for a while. The situation of Surat is picturesque, on the river Tapti and not on the open sea. The river was wide at the point of the factory's location, and it must have been considered a safe and comfortable berth for ships. The factory and some other buildings of the period were substantial and afforded a broad view of the river and the farther shore.

When the Company established further outposts, the land on which they stood was leased or ceded to them by the local rulers. It was found that the deterioration of Mogul rule had caused such disorder in the country that it was difficult to trade peacefully. The result was that additional land around the trading post was frequently acquired by gift or purchase, defenses were set up, and sometimes a small detachment of men, both English and Indian, was set to guard the warehouse and maintain law and order. In some posts Indian merchants moved into these settlements for safety and convenience in trading. At Fort St. George, Madras, 250,000 Indians established themselves in the new town.

The romantic beginning of Bombay is well known. The small island and fishing village of that name were part of the dowry of Catherine of Braganza (Portugal) on her marriage to Charles II of England in 1660. It was a grand gesture which at the time seemed quite useless from a practical point of view. Bombay, however, had an excellent natural harbor and has been developed into one of the great cities of the world, which in various ways may remind the traveler of New York.

In 1690 the city of Calcutta was established by Job Charnock on the east bank of the Ganges. A few years later the land nearby was also ceded, and Fort William was built. Job Charnock was a picturesque pioneer. The date of his birth is not known, but he came to India on his own in 1655 or 1656 and soon joined the East India Company. He was the sort of person around whom legends and traditions gather, and it is said that his wife was a young and beautiful Hindu widow whom he had rescued from her husband's funeral pyre. They had several children, and he mourned her deeply when she died. Charnock himself died in 1693.

About this time the French were seriously turning their attention to India. Troubled waters always invite adventurous fishing, and the French were fully aware of the collapse of the Mogul regime.

78

There were three causes for the fall of Mogul power:

First the Moguls had remained outsiders. Akbar was the only one of his line who identified himself with India and attempted to build up a united nation.

Second, the Mogul armies were vast, ill-trained rabbles. Eventually both the French and English enlisted Indian infantrymen (sepoys), and though they were generally described as "half-disciplined," they demonstrated the valor and soldierly qualities which later placed the Indian army among the finest troops in the world. Even when they were first recruited, however, they showed how well a small body of disciplined men could hold their own against huge but unorganized forces.

Third, the reckless extravagance of the Moguls in maintaining their pomp and show was ultimately seen to be carried on at the expense of the peasantry.

March-past of the Camel Corps is a highlight of many celebrations

The Marathas

As the East India Company gradually spread its domains, two rebellions with religious motivation took place: the Maratha and the Sikh. The Marathas who seized power in western India swept across the country as far as Delhi; they were ardently Hindu and in the name of religion determined to extirpate what was left of Muslim rule. They were not interested in administration but in seizing what they could in raids and then establishing themselves in the hills of western India. The Maratha Confederacy was defeated by the English at Panipat—an historic battleground. Following the collapse of the Confederacy, the Central India States were plagued for some time by freebooters such as the Pindaris and Thugs.

Under such circumstances people lived by their wits, and rajahs (Hindu princes) in various parts of the country used every wile at their command to play off the foreigners against one another, ceding or selling or transferring lands and privileges until both the French and the English were in possession of considerable territories as a base for trade. The two European nations fought it out between them until in 1763 the French withdrew to a large extent from India.

The Sikhs

Nanak, the son of a grain dealer in Lahore, Punjab, was deeply impressed by Kabir the weaver-saint of the fifteenth century and became his follower. Nanak, like his master, wished to build a bridge between Hinduism and Islam.

"God has declared," he said, "that He will not ask a man his tribe or sect, but what he has done."

Nanak spread his teaching in the Punjab, and there his followers became known as Sikhs, or learners. As the sect grew, it was centered in the city of Amritsar where the Golden Temple is now visited by many tourists. Under a succession of leaders known as *Gurus* the Sikhs developed a semimilitary organization which did not keep caste; they became distinct from both Hindus and Muslims. Sikhs are widely known for their military bearing and their long hair. Every Sikh keeps the

80

Sikh Golden Temple at Amritsar in northern India

"five K's," which may be translated as long hair, comb, shorts, dagger, and iron bracelet. Their sacred book, the Granth, is the object of intense veneration.

Their hero, Ranjit Singh, like some other men famous in Indian history, became a leader at the age of twelve, in 1792. In 1849 the so-called Sikh nation finally became part of India, which was now largely administered by the East India Company. Later they were to win world-wide fame as an important part of the Indian army. They have also served as police in international centers such as Hongkong and—formerly—Shanghai.

John Company Hands Over

In 1857 occurred the Sepoy Revolt, also called by some writers the Indian Mutiny and by others, a Revolution. As a consequence of this crisis the East India Company ended the anomalous situation of their rule and gave way to the Crown. Queen Victoria was proclaimed Empress of India. Her proclamation in 1858 is generally acknowledged to be a remarkable document. She assured the people of India of just government and complete freedom of religion, and the ensuing Pax Britannica gave India a unity, peace, and tranquility which she had never known before. The days of Akbar are the only comparable period. This latest conquest of India was initiated and carried on by the pen, and though the sword played its part on occasion, it was an army of clerks and scholars who built up the last of the Indian empires that finally gave way to the Republic of India, member of the Commonwealth and of the United Nations Organization.

It is seldom realized that not all of India came under direct British rule. About one-third of the territory and one-quarter of the population remained in Indian states, governed by maharajahs or nawabs, except for external affairs. Some of these states were enterprising and modern in their outlook with democratic institutions; others were typically feudal. The larger states and groups of smaller states had resident British advisers, but within the state the ruler enjoyed complete power and control of the revenue. The communications systems of India (postal, telegraph, and railway) were used by the states, though some had their own currency and postage stamps for internal use.

The reorganization of the country was a tremendous undertaking. For example, roads in the modern sense of the word were almost nonexistent. From ancient times there had been some roads along which the vast, cumbersome armies could move. There are four great highways stretching diagonally across the country, which have been in existence for a long time and are rich in historical associations. The most famous is the ancient marching route, the Grand Trunk Road, which is familiar to Western readers from *Kim* and other stories of India. This road stretches across the north of India (and now of Pakistan) from Calcutta to the Khyber Pass. The other three roads connect Bombay with Delhi, Calcutta with Madras, and Madras with Bombay, about five thousand miles in all.

These roads had to be modernized, and many others had to be created, with the necessary bridges and travelers' rest houses. Building roads helped greatly in establishing law and order in the country, and of course the time came when they were a necessity for motor transport; trucks and buses are now a familiar sight and have largely taken the place of the oxcart. There are now half a million miles of roads in India.

Railways were planned in the first instance to secure the movement of grain from one part of the country to another and thus to control famine, but railways now play the same part in India as they do in other countries of great distances. The first railway in India dates from 1853, which may be compared with 1825 in England, 1830 in the United States, and 1836 in Canada. India now has the second largest railway system in the world with a total of thirty-six thousand miles. Nearly five million passengers are carried daily, and over 1,200,000 people are employed by the railways of India.

The first survey of India was set up in 1767, and it has become an important department of government, producing aerial surveys and reliable maps as well as other services. But the survey also entered into the lives of many people. For the first time the headmen of the villages were expected to know with some degree of accuracy the boundaries of their villages and of the family holdings in it.

Here we see how difficult it is to govern another people, and how mistakes may be made with the best intentions. In the eighteenth century many villages owned the land around them corporately. At the death of the head of a family the land reverted either to the village unit or to the ruler—"The king is every man's heir" was the expression used—and it was then redistributed. Such a system was difficult for the British to understand. They were a nation of land lovers, and their system was based on individual ownership. When they tried to organize a "permanent settlement" in India, the scheme aroused suspicion and hostility. The other mistake was in regard to a class of major landowners, the *zemindars,* found in some parts of the country, whom the British took to be similar to their own squires. The *zemindars* were given recognition and were asked to collect taxes for the government, keeping a due percentage for themselves. The system was not a success and was eventually abolished, but not before it had created some hostility.

Over the country as a whole the district officer was the key man of the administration. He was a member of the civil service and combined the duties of revenue collector and magistrate. These duties required him to be constantly on the go, meeting the people of his district on their own ground at least three weeks in a month, studying the problems on the spot, and doing what he could for the welfare of his people. For example, if the rains had been scanty and the crops poor, he could secure a modification or even a remission of the taxes for the year; if necessary he started famine relief works and brought in grain. Perhaps the best summary of the collector's duties may be found in the instructions of Sir Henry Lawrence over a century ago to his young men when he sent them out to their surprisingly large districts: their orders were to "settle the country, make the people happy, and take care there are no rows."

The Indian civil service was justly regarded as a distinguished corps of civil servants. At first its members were all British, but as modern education developed, Indians in increasing numbers took the qualifying examinations with the result that when independence was achieved in 1947, the majority of civil servants were Indians, and there was consequently no breakdown in the administration of the country during the period of transition which followed the end of British rule. The men and women who constitute the Indian administrative service are highly intelligent, well trained, and dedicated.

Not all Englishmen were able to foresee the dawn of self-determination for India, at least until the time was near, but there were a few who had clearer vision and were able to dream a great dream. Such was Lord Moira (governor-general 1814 to 1823) who foretold that it would be a great day when "India could walk alone in the paths of justice." Macaulay's statement has been often quoted, "Whenever it comes, it will be the proudest day in English history."

But governments, especially democratic governments, do not extend from the top downward. It is necessary for the people to become politically conscious. Under the British a middle class came into being in both rural and urban areas. This new class took to modern education which offered new opportunities in many fields. Surprisingly, public funds were set aside for education in India before they were so allocated in Britain. In 1850 Lord Dalhousie started an education system for the whole of India. After much discussion the emphasis was laid on English rather than on the classical Sanskrit as the medium of instruction in secondary and higher education. This was done in order to link India with the rapid and important developments that were taking place in science.

One result of the introduction of English was that for the first time India had the use of a language in which educated persons from different parts of the country could communicate with one another. The multiplicity of languages was reserved for domestic and daily use, and regional languages were taught in elementary schools, but now the Aryan and the Dravidian could talk with one another. What Latin did for Europe during many centuries, English did for India. Not only did

Elephants on parade in front of government buildings at New Delhi

English provide an important means of communication, but the introduction of English literature with the humanism and liberalism of the period did much for the thinking of the younger men. Of Gokhale, an outstanding liberal and social reformer (1842 to 1901), we are told that in his college days he memorized entire speeches by Burke and other British orators, and also the whole of Milton's "Paradise Lost."

The Indian National Congress

With these ideas fermenting in men's minds and the provision of a common language for educated people, the organization of the Indian National Congress in 1883 was as significant as it was timely. (The word "Congress" in this connection means a convention or conference, not an instrument of government as in the United States.)

The suggestion for this organization came from Allan Octavian Hume, a civil servant who had retired in the land he loved. It marked the beginning of a new era, not only in India but in the history of political evolution. The Indian National Congress became the training ground for the birth of the Indian nation. It was distinguished from its inception by leadership of great ability and moderation.

The tremendous vitality of the awakening Indian nation showed itself in many forms. Courageous attempts at social reform at times rivaled political aspirations and threatened to split the Congress, but a Social Reform Conference was eventually organized as a parallel to the Congress. Ardent Congressmen felt that political reform must come first and that social matters could be attended to later. Social Reformers held, however, that it was essential for India to put her house in order. Some outstanding men such as Gokhale belonged to both organizations, but there was no real attempt to blend the two strains until Gandhi brought forward his program of civil disobedience on the one hand and what he called his constructive program on the other.

It is unfortunate that to many non-Indians Gandhi appears like a meteor flashing across the recent history of India. Actually, he was in himself the culmination of much that had been developing for a generation or more and an interpreter of his own times. A student of the life and work of Bal Gangadhar Tilak of western India, generally known as Lokmanya (1856 to 1920), will find that he initiated several ideas and forms of propaganda which were later identified with Gandhi. It was Tilak who gave the battle cry for the independence movement, "Swaraj (self-rule) is my birthright and I will have it." Civil disobedience and the boycott of foreign goods were weapons advocated by Tilak and later developed by Gandhi. But Tilak thought that social reform could wait. Many persons disagreed with him, for their aim was to produce a nation fit for democracy.

Mahatma Gandhi

Mohandas Karamchand Gandhi (1869 to 1948) was born in a middle caste. His father and grandfather had both been prime ministers of a state in Gujerat, western India. He received an average Indian education and then went to London to qualify as a barrister-at-law. While in London he saw the struggles of the suffragettes to win the franchise for women. Their methods were forms of civil disobedience. He also saw the acceptance of the principle of the right of labor unions to strike. Both these events are possible factors in his thinking. When he returned to India, he encountered the philosophy of civil disobedience as set forth by Tilak. Yet other factors entered the situation, until in time Gandhi had forged a political weapon out of the concept of civil disobedience.

He had not been long in India after his return when he received a professional call to South Africa. There he stayed for several years, and during that time two different influences molded his thinking. One was the racial discrimination he observed and experienced. The other was a group of writers to whom he owed much.

Gandhi read Ruskin, who in *Unto This Last* dealt with principles of political economy. Later Gandhi referred to this book as having "marked a turning point" in his life. Thoreau's "Essay on Civil Disobedience" gave Gandhi a "sense of kinship." Both Gandhi and Thoreau had been in prison for practicing civil disobedience; both had studied the *Bhagavad Gita* and other books of Hindu philosophy. The third

The President's House in New Delhi is bright with lights to celebrate Republic Day

writer who helped Gandhi to think out his principles was Leo Tolstoy, author of *The Kingdom of God is Within You.* We must also mention that before Gandhi went to South Africa, during his stay there, and after his return to India, he was an earnest student of the New Testament, especially the Sermon on the Mount. Thus Gandhi set out on his search for a way of life that would contain many diverse elements. To the end he was a seeker, or as he wrote, "The throne of my heart has remained vacant and my search still continues."

It is not necessary to trace Gandhi's career in detail, for it is well known. He achieved an agreement with the government of South Africa regarding the position of Indians in South Africa. When he returned to India, he took up the cause of labor in Bihar and became involved in Congress activities and politics, which became almost entirely concerned with the struggle for independence. From time to time Gandhi

88

launched a civil disobedience campaign, as he found it an effective weapon. From time to time also he fasted, as an act of purification or atonement or even of spiritual power. He became convinced that both forms of protest required special preparation of mind and spirit, and he did not always give permission for his followers to use them. He claimed that fasting and civil disobedience were weapons too potent for those who did not know how to use them.

When political emancipation was in sight, he turned his attention more and more to social problems and spent his last months in endeavoring to heal the wounds that the partition of the country at the time of independence had caused. It was resentment of his efforts in this connection that led to an extreme rightist group taking action to end his life.

It will probably be many years before a definitive appraisal can be made of Gandhi's life and work. Until then he remains, as he did in life, a controversial figure. Certainly he was a man of paradoxes. For example, he deliberately broke some of the rules of the caste system, and he constantly preached and practiced brotherliness and kindness to the outcastes for whom he invented the kindlier term *Harijan*, the people of God. Nevertheless he continued to accept caste as a system.

Perhaps one of the most striking features about Gandhi is the influence his ideas and methods have had abroad, especially in the United States where he has acquired almost legendary significance, as may be seen from the references to Gandhi by the leaders of the Negro civil rights movement.

It has often been asked, "Was Gandhi the saint in politics or the politician trying to be a saint?" Who can say? But his undisputed title in India is the "Father of the Nation."

Under his disciple and successor, Jawaharlal Nehru, India moved with dignity to take her rightful place among the nations of the world.

A village market is always a beehive of activity

Caste: The Great Beehive

When Ted and Jim, fellow students at an American university, were on their way to visit India, a pleasant traveling companion was Chandra, an Indian student on his way home after studying abroad. He gave his new friends a warm invitation to visit him in Gopalpur. A few weeks later Ted and Jim had completed the usual tourist tour program and were able to pay the promised visit.

Gopalpur could be described as either a large village or a small town. It was situated just off a main highway a few miles away from an industrial city. Chandra's father, Laxman, owned a good deal of land in and near Gopalpur, and his large, old-fashioned house was a comfortable place in which to stay, though it was always overflowing with relations and friends. The hospitality of the family was warm and seemed to be boundless.

Ted and Jim had greatly enjoyed seeing some of the famous places in India, but now they were glad to sit down, sort out their impressions, and ask questions about things that had puzzled them. As Chandra had been abroad himself, he readily understood how difficult it might be to understand a social setting different from one's own. The boys found him helpful in answering their questions.

What Is Caste?

One evening they said to him that the biggest question they wanted to ask was about caste. What *was* caste and how did it work? They had tried to find out by observation on their travels, but they were still confused.

Chandra said, "I don't think you can understand caste as well in big cities, such as those you have been visiting, as in a village like this, where in spite of a certain amount of modernization the old pattern of life can be clearly seen. Let's begin by looking at the layout of the village. When you went to find something in the brass bazaar, what did you notice?"

"I remember noticing that all the brass shops and the metalworkers were in one street," said Ted.

"And when I wanted to buy a piece of cloth for a shirt, all the cloth shops were together in another street," said Jim.

Ted took a piece of paper and began to make a rough map of the village; it was soon evident that most people lived in neighborhoods grouped together according to their business or professional interests. In the next few days the boys explored the village thoroughly and brought their questions to Chandra.

Caste Is a Pattern for Living

"If a carpenter thinks he would like to live in another part of the village, what would he do?"

"He wouldn't do anything," said Chandra. "He knows he wouldn't be welcome elsewhere, and he would miss his old friends."

"Suppose his son got some new ideas and wanted to move?"

"He might do so in the city, especially if he had a different profession from his father's. Here it isn't very likely. A carpenter's son almost always becomes a carpenter. He works with his father from the time he is a boy until he has learned all about the trade and can eventually take over."

"At home people often say to a boy, 'What do you want to be when you grow up?' I guess there is not much use saying that here," observed Ted.

"Oh, there is a good deal of choice nowadays," said Chandra, "but not as much as in England or America. The important thing is first to get as much education as you can, and then keep your eyes open for a chance. It is surprising how many opportunities turn up. But of course it is easier if the rules of caste don't interfere."

"After all," said Jim, "the people who made the rules in the old days had no idea how things would develop."

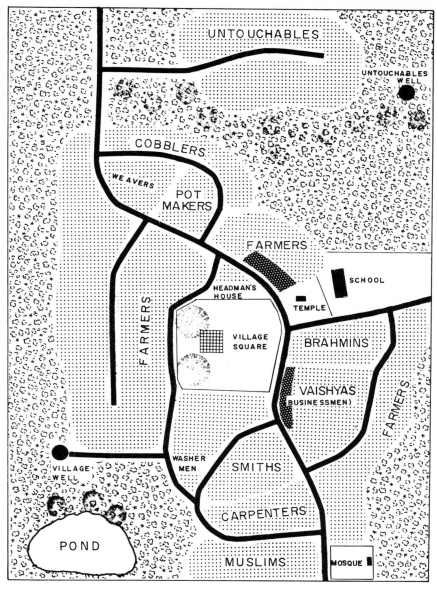

UNTOUCHABLES

UNTOUCHABLES WELL

COBBLERS

WEAVERS

POT MAKERS

FARMERS

FARMERS

HEADMAN'S HOUSE

SCHOOL

TEMPLE

VILLAGE SQUARE

BRAHMINS

FARMERS

VAISHYAS (BUSINESSMEN)

VILLAGE WELL

WASHER MEN

SMITHS

CARPENTERS

POND

MUSLIMS

MOSQUE

 RESIDENTIAL

 COMMERCIAL

AS SHOWN INSTITUTIONAL

AGRICULTURAL

Basket-makers at work by the roadside

"That's true," said Chandra.

He was silent for a few minutes, and then said, "But there are other important features about caste and village life." Feeling carefully for the right words that would help his friends to understand, Chandra continued, "It is partly a system of barter; goods and services are not so much bought as *exchanged*. It is what we call *jajmani*, and there is something friendly and cooperative about this way of doing things. The system started hundreds of years ago when money as we know it didn't exist. Later when coins were made, few if any came to a village like this. Even the taxes were paid in grain."

"What did people do without money?" asked Ted.

"What they still do now, except of course for the taxes," said Chandra. "You have seen people of many castes coming in and out of our house or courtyard. Just yesterday the blacksmith came to see my father about having the work oxen reshod. The carpenter put up a shelf.

The weaver brought my mother a bolt of cloth, and the potter brought some pots she had asked him to make. You know I shave myself just as you do, but my father is shaved by the village barber every morning. Have you seen any of these workers paid in cash?"

"No, but they must earn something."

"Of course they do, and when harvest comes in, about three months from now, they will all get their fair share of grain for the year, and perhaps some cloth too. When there is a big event, like a wedding in the family, everyone comes in to help according to his capacity and is similarly rewarded."

"Now that I think of it," said Ted, "I remember my father telling me that when my grandfather, who was a farmer, was building a barn, all the neighbors came to help him 'raise the roof' as they called it. And my grandmother used to take butter and eggs from her dairy and chickens and exchange them at the village shop for things she wanted but couldn't produce on the farm."

Chandra looked pleased. "That was a kind of *jajmani,* I should say."

"Yes," said Jim, "but it didn't last. In one or two generations in America barter had gone. In India it seems to have lasted a very long time and become combined with other factors."

Once more Ted had been busy with his pencil. Now he looked up and said, "I think I understand it now. Caste in the village is just one huge beehive, or honeycomb—whichever you may want to call it. Each little cell is quite separate, but it has walls and each wall touches a wall of another cell. In the same way each caste is separate and distinct, but they are all dependent upon one another, and you couldn't take one or two away without affecting the whole system."

The boys took Ted's drawing to Laxman who looked at it with interest.

"I never thought of it that way before," he said, "but I think you have the right idea. Caste both unites people and separates them. Many people have claimed that it has given them a sense of security because they have known just where they belonged on the social ladder, and they were sure of the support of their fellow caste members. On the other hand there are mutual obligations between different sections of society. Where caste has gone wrong is in being rigid and expecting people to fit into molds which are decided for them by birth and not by ability or choice. Well, we must learn how to live as individuals and yet cooperate with other people to build a secure society. It is you young ones who will have to discover how to do that."

Caste and Marriage

A few days later the boys noticed that there was even more than the usual number of visitors, and a good deal of talking and consulting was going on. Jim and Ted asked what it was all about, but Chandra only laughed and said, "My father will tell you."

One afternoon, after the visitors had gone, Laxman was sitting quietly alone on his veranda enjoying a peaceful pipe. When he saw that Ted and Jim appeared to have nothing special to do, he beckoned them to come and sit with him. They felt honored by the invitation of the older man. At first they talked about local news and about the crops, then Laxman said, "Perhaps you have been wondering about the visitors we have had lately."

The boys were rather embarrassed, hoping they had not shown undue curiosity, but admitted that it was so. Laxman said kindly, "It is quite all right. Anybody would wonder what was brewing. As a matter of fact, we were discussing plans for Chandra's marriage."

The boys looked so astonished that Laxman had to laugh.

"But why doesn't Chandra decide the matter for himself?" Jim asked.

"Of course if the girl is willing," Ted added hastily.

"No," said Laxman, "we don't think it is a matter to be left entirely to the young people. You see, we think the group we belong to is very important, first the family group and then the caste. The welfare of the individual depends largely on the welfare of the group; on the other hand the welfare of the group depends on that of each family in the group. Such an important thing as marriage affects many people besides the young couple. In other words, marriage is to a large extent governed by the rules of our caste."

A potter spins bowls on his wheel in the Punjab

"What!" exclaimed Ted. "Caste decides your occupation and now you say that it decides your marriage also!"

"Yes," said Laxman, "and even more often than it decides occupation. We must marry within our caste but outside the clan which is a subdivision of the caste. So," continued Laxman, "we have been looking for a suitable girl for Chandra, and we think we have found one. Some members of her family and a mutual friend came to discuss business matters with us, and they brought her horoscope and family records. Probably the wedding will take place soon after the harvest. We hope you will be able to attend."

"Thank you, sir. But, Chandra, did you have nothing to say to all this?"

"Oh, yes," said Chandra cheerfully, "my father is quite modern about such things. He asked my opinion some time ago, and I have even had a look at the girl and thought she was quite pretty! As a matter of fact she is a friend of one of my sisters, and I have met

97

her several times. She has also had quite a good education. I know that my father has my interests at heart, and he is doing his best to make sure of a happy future for me."

How Did Caste Begin?

About a week later the boys had some more questions to ask, and again a conversation developed when they were sitting with Laxman and Chandra on the veranda.

"How many castes are there?" inquired Jim.

"There are said to be over three thousand," replied Laxman, "but census enumerators have stopped recording them, so it is impossible to be accurate. Moreover, from time to time, new castes split off from old ones, and may be called subcastes."

"How did this caste business start?" asked Ted.

Nobody knows, the boys were told, because it began a very long

Weaver using a handloom in northern India

time ago, perhaps about three thousand years. When the Aryan tribes moved into India, they had at first three and later on four classes, called *varna,* who divided the responsibility and the work among them. The early Aryans had a strong belief in law and order, or natural and moral law, as they would say. They expressed it in a picturesque way when they said that the four *varna* came from the body of the Creator. From his head came the Brahmans, the priests, whose duty it was to offer the sacrifices and chant the sacred hymns. The Kshatriyas, the warriors, sprang from his shoulders, and of course it was their duty to defend the tribe. From his thighs came the artisans and agriculturists, the Vaisyas, who looked after the production and trade of the tribe. From the Creator's feet came the Sudras who did the unskilled work of the community. It is probable that the Sudras were older inhabitants of the land who were pressed into service by the Aryans.

Scholars, both Indian and Western, have different theories about caste, but perhaps the best way to talk about it is to refer to the original four *varnas* as classes, and all the many other subdivisions that took place as castes, or *jati.*

Factors in Caste Development

When the Aryans arrived in India, they met the Dravidians who had been there a long time and who had developed a social structure. The two kinds of tribes, Aryan and Dravidian, did not assimilate, which is not surprising when we remember that they came of different ethnic stock, had different social customs, and worshipped different gods. It seemed natural for the Aryans and Dravidians to wish to keep apart, and even now race, language, religion, and customs tend to divide the people of this country between north and south.

Chandra said, "Geography is a factor too in the development of caste. Our country is divided by many physical features—the rivers and mountains, deep valleys, jungles and forests. Before there were good roads, it was easy for people to live more or less in isolation, so they developed their own local culture and were afraid of strangers."

Chandra turned to his father. "Do you remember the man who

visited us last year who had done considerable traveling in the lower hills of the Himalayas? He explored one of the river valleys, and there he found a number of villages. He also found that the inhabitants of these village settlements would visit and trade with each other by going up and down the valley, following the course of the river, but not one of them had ever climbed the ridge on either side or discovered the people who lived in the next valley."

"So occupation, marriage, and place of residence are all factors in observing caste," remarked Ted.

"There is one more, no less important," smiled Chandra, "and that is food."

"Food?" exclaimed both boys in surprise.

"Yes, indeed," said Laxman, "the kind of food, who prepares it, and where you eat it, all are very important. Even the gods can be divided into vegetarian and nonvegetarian. There are high gods who are served by vegetarian priests, the Brahmans. Other gods, and especially village goddesses have animal sacrifices and non-Brahman priests. Hindus will not eat beef though some eat mutton; the higher castes usually eat no meat at all, though some Brahmans will eat fish. Indeed, food habits and taboos are a convenient way of grading the various castes in the village."

"Please tell us more about the different castes," said Jim. "Are there many in this village?"

Chandra and Laxman began to count them off for the benefit of their guests.

Castes in the Village

First to be mentioned were the Brahmans, the priests, of whom there were only four in the village as there was not much for them to do. In the old days they usually taught the village school which was held in or near the temple. Now all the children went to government schools which were in modern buildings, and the teachers were trained men and women of any caste. Nowadays the Brahmans were responsible only for the daily worship in the temple and for performing mar-

100

riages and other rituals. Most of the people in the village were farmers and shepherds. Since there was no one of the warrior caste in the village, the farmer ranked high, next to the Brahman. The shopkeepers, some of whom were moneylenders, were quite important. Then there were a number of artisan castes who were not all of the same rank. Carpenters and blacksmiths, for example, ranked higher than potters and weavers. Lower still were the stoneworkers who prepared the stones for road construction, the makers of baskets, and the families who extracted vegetable oils. The leatherworkers were regarded as quite low in the scale. Altogether there were about fifteen castes in the small village of about 500 people who lived in 120 families.

Caste hierarchy varies in different parts of the country. A man who is of low caste in one village may be an outcaste elsewhere, or in one place a Brahman will have the most influence while in another place it will be an industrialist.

"How do you know what caste people belong to?" inquired Jim. "Do you ask them?"

Home of a prosperous farmer in rural India

"Sometimes we do," replied Laxman, "though we prefer not to ask. Frequently a man's caste is revealed by his name, his manner, and his appearance. In the case of women the kind of clothes and jewelry they wear tell us a good deal."

Jim and Ted became more observant after that and began to notice significant differences among the people they met. It was easier to notice variations between castes in a village than in a city, because old customs linger longer in a rural setting.

In Gopalpur Ted and Jim noticed that frequently men would get off their bicycles to greet Laxman, even though no conversation might follow the exchange of greetings. When Ted inquired why it was necessary for a man to dismount just to say, "How are you?" he was told that it was a sign of respect to Laxman on the part of a man of lower caste. In the old days an outcaste was not allowed to ride a horse, and later when there was more freedom about social restrictions, the rider would dismount when passing an important person. In south India at one time there were detailed regulations as to the distance an outcaste must keep from a caste man, say fifty feet. Such regulations are no longer observed, but there is still evident in some people a timidity about social approach that suggests their caste.

Bearing, facial expression, language, variations in dress, and many details too numerous to mention are often indications to the expert eye of the type of person he is meeting. Modern life is smoothing out many differences, but some will probably linger for a long time, so entrenched have they become as social habits.

A Visit to the Harijans

One day the boys came upon a section of the village set apart from all the other houses. When they asked about it, they were told that it was where the Harijans, or outcastes, lived. None of Laxman's family ever went there, but Chandra said he knew a young Harijan who had gone to college. Chandra had met him in the city.

"I'll send for Bhima and introduce you," he said. "But I must ask you one thing. If you visit Bhima's home, please be sure to take a

Plowing in the old way with oxen

bath before you come back into our house, or my mother will not feel happy."

"Why, will our visit make us so dirty?" asked the boys in surprise.

"No, not what you would call 'dirty,' but to an orthodox person you will be defiled by having associated with outcaste people, perhaps even accepting refreshments from them, so you will be 'ritually impure,' and you should bathe and put on clean clothes before rejoining the family." There was a convenient bathhouse built outside Laxman's house, so they readily agreed to use it after visiting Bhima's village.

Bhima proved to be a friendly outgoing chap who was able to talk with them in English, and they went to visit his home and neighbors.

Jim and Ted discovered that some of the people in that section had rather unattractive occupations. Some of them cleaned the streets of the village, and others looked after the sanitation which was quite primitive. The boys asked what would happen if they refused to do this work. Bhima agreed that it would upset the village economy and

Transporting cotton from the fields to the mills near Delhi

way of life very badly. Ultimately, of course, modern sanitation would come to the village as it had to the city, and the situation would be vastly improved. Others in the Harijan section were leatherworkers; their occupation included skinning dead animals, tanning hides, and manufacturing footwear. Again, some Harijans made baskets and others processed vegetable oils.

"But why should any of you be compelled to do this kind of work? On the other hand, why should there be any disgrace in making such useful things as shoes and sandals?" persisted the boys.

Bhima replied, "According to the Hindu doctrine of *karma* we did not lead good lives in our previous time on earth, so we did not earn a good place in this life. If we live better now, things will improve for us next time."

"Is that what you believe yourself?" asked Ted.

"No, frankly it isn't. But after all we are a minority, though not a small one, and it is what other people believe about us that counts."

Bhima explained to them that several names were used for his kind of people. The old terms were "outcaste," "untouchable," or "pariah," but Gandhi had introduced the term "Harijan" which means "people of God," and that is the polite expression in general use. Government officers and papers, however, use the expression "scheduled castes."

Not all the Harijans had to do despised tasks. Many of them were becoming educated, and quite a number went to the city every day by bus or bicycle or even on foot; they worked in the mills there or had some other employment. Like Bhima some who were bright and ambitious were going into politics. Aside from the small area where hides were tanned, the general appearance of the Harijan quarters was clean and attractive. The people had their own wells and sanitation. They now had the right to use a public well but preferred to have their own if possible. Since 1950 when the new Constitution went into effect, it was no longer permissible to discriminate against anyone on the grounds of caste, creed, race, or sex. The Harijans were proud of their rights as citizens and very much aware of them.

Bullocks pull a load of cow-dung cakes that will be used for fuel

Bhima spoke about their great leader, Dr. Bhimrao Ambedkar, who had taught them that they had not always been a despised people. According to his historical research the Harijans were descendants of people who had at one time ruled much of India. In the conflicts that took place between the invaders and the older inhabitants, it sometimes happened that bands of defenders lost their leaders. They became what were known as leaderless or "broken" men. They had to make what terms they could with the conquerors, who usually assigned the defeated men land outside the bounds of the village proper and gave them permission to earn their livelihood in any noncompetitive way that would not disturb the village economy.

Bhima told Jim and Ted the fascinating story of the life of Dr. Ambedkar, who had died only a few years previously. As a small boy Ambedkar was eager for an education, so he joined a primary school near his home. As he was the only outcaste pupil, he was not permitted in the classroom but sat on the veranda where he could see the blackboard; occasionally the teacher would stroll over and ask him a question or two. When young Ambedkar got to high school, things were better, for there were several other outcaste boys with similar ambitions, and they sat together on the back bench of the classroom. College days were better still, and Ambedkar attracted some attention, as he was the first outcaste boy to graduate with a B.A. from the University of Bombay. He was rewarded by a scholarship which enabled him to go to England, Europe, and America; ten years later he returned to India with three doctoral degrees. He had also been admitted as a barrister-at-law in London.

Ambedkar never forgot the people from whom he had come, and during his distinguished career in public life he fought for them and their rights. When independence came to India in 1947, Dr. Ambedkar became Minister of Law, and in that capacity he piloted the new Constitution through the House of Parliament.

Bhima's eyes shone as he quoted the Preamble to the Constitution of India, which begins with the words "We, the People of India" and goes on to promise justice, liberty, equality, and fraternity to all the citizens of India.

Primitive village well. Buckets are made of leather

Ted and Jim went back to Laxman's home in a very thoughtful mood. What does democracy mean in a country like India in transition from ancient ways to an honored place among the nations of the world? They remembered the last thing Bhima had said to them.

"We have our guaranteed rights. Nobody can take them away from us. But no laws can make people like us or respect us; we have to earn that ourselves, and we are making progress. It is more difficult to see progress in the village, perhaps, because people are more set in their ways here, and there is no point in upsetting them more than necessary. But"—his face broke into a broad smile—"you should have seen what fun Chandra and I used to have in college when we got together there."

A village school—old-fashioned but useful

Ramesh and Grandfather Go to School

One day there was a stranger in the village. Ramesh stopped his play long enough to follow him like a little shadow. Grandfather looked up from his pipe, and his eyes too followed the stranger. When Ramesh's father came home from the field, both Ramesh and Grandfather asked him who the stranger was and why he was wandering around. Ramesh's father laughed. "Why, he's the new school-teacher. Didn't you know we were going to have a new school? That's the building over there, the one we have been working on in our spare time. The walls are nearly up, and pretty soon someone from the government will send us some corrugated iron sheets for the roof, and then when the rains are over, we shall be ready to open the new school."

It turned out just as Father said, and soon there was a fine new school packed with youngsters both boys and girls, and not one but three teachers, one of them a woman. Nobody had thought of sending the girls of the village to school, but when the pretty schoolmistress appeared, it seemed quite natural for the girls to go to school, too. Of course Ramesh enrolled, and every morning Grandfather followed him to school and sat in the shade outside and listened to what was going on.

One of the teachers noticed him, and one day at recess time he walked over to see Grandfather, saluted him respectfully, and then listened to the host of questions Grandfather fired at him. Finally he laughed and said, "Why don't you come to school yourself, sir, since you are so interested in it?"

Grandfather looked hurt, "A nice fool I'd look at my age," he said, "but I certainly wish I had had the chance when I was a boy."

The teacher said, "Evidently you haven't heard about the new class we are going to start next week, which will be only for grown-ups."

"What's this? What's this?" said Grandfather, scarcely believing his ears. "Nay, Mr. Schoolmaster, don't make fun of an old man."

"But I'm not making fun of you," replied the schoolmaster. "Don't you know ten of the older men of the village have enrolled already? I'm sure you would have heard of it if you hadn't been away at a family wedding."

"Tell me more," said Grandfather.

And so it happened that in the evening, after the day's work was over, the senior schoolmaster used to start his class for grown-up people, and not only men but several women came too. The charts and books they had were quite different from those the children used and contained material that was interesting to them. A few of the older people had once learned to read but had had nothing to read and practice on, no books or magazines or newspapers, so they had forgotten, but they soon picked it up again. One of the first things that Grandfather learned to do was to write his name, and that made

An adult education student receiving an award

Peace Corps Volunteer teaching in a boys' multipurpose school

him feel very important. "Now," said the teacher, "you can sign a receipt or a letter, and it will be useful in many ways. You are an important person, Grandfather, and you should be able to write your own name."

One of the other men found difficulty in seeing some of the letters in the reading book and almost gave up. But Grandfather said to him, "Why don't you take the bus into town and get yourself a pair of spectacles? Then it would be much easier for you to read and write, and you would see all sorts of things you haven't noticed for a long time."

"That's just what I will do," said his friend, and a few days later he came to class with a fine pair of spectacles perched on his nose.

Perhaps the thing that pleased Grandfather as much as anything happened the day he heard Ramesh make a mistake in his reading. When Grandfather was able to point it out to him, he really did give himself airs!

A girl teaches her stepmother, who is not much older than she, to read

Each One Teach One

After the class had been going on for several months and a number of the older men and women had learned to read, a day was fixed when they would get their certificates and prizes to celebrate the fact that they were now readers. The village people made quite an event of the occasion; they put up some decorations in the village square and spread rugs where the visitors they were expecting could sit. They put a special rug to one side for the adults who had learned to read.

Several people came out from the city, some of them government officers and others social workers and citizens who were interested in the literacy movement which taught adults to read.

After the certificates and prizes had been distributed and before the refreshments were served, one of the most important visitors made a speech. He explained how necessary it was that every person in India should be able to read. He also explained that it was such a big job to teach almost the whole country that progress would be slow if people waited for the government to do it all. But, he said, there was one good way that had been a great success in other parts of India and in some other countries too. That was "Each one teach one." Every single person who received a certificate that day could teach someone else, and that person would teach someone else, and all the readers would keep on teaching someone else, and—Ramesh's head began to feel dizzy in trying to do all the sums involved in finding out how many people would read and how soon. But Grandfather nodded, and began choosing in his mind the people he would begin to teach.

This simple but effective method was the discovery of an American missionary, Dr. Frank Laubach, who has become world famous as "the apostle of the illiterates." About 1935 he first visited India, and

Grandfather learns how to read

many people there caught a vision of what literacy could mean to India and to the world.

Just when the gathering was about to disperse, a telegraph messenger came into the village and began to ask for someone. Each person he asked pointed to Grandfather. To Grandfather's great surprise the telegraph man came to him, handed him a telegram, and asked him to sign the receipt for it. It was the first time Grandfather had ever had a telegram, but he signed the receipt with his name quite boldly. Then he opened the telegram. It was from one of his nephews in the city who had heard of Grandfather's achievement. The telegram read "Congratulations we are proud of you." And Grandfather read it entirely himself.

Democracy and Literacy

This simple incident of Grandfather and Ramesh may be multiplied many times in India today, for the country is hungry and thirsty for education as never before. It has not, however, been a sudden, inexplicable growth, but one that has gradually been planned for and de-

College girls performing a folk dance

Students watching sports. Saris are useful as sunshades

veloped for over a century, though the rate of progress has much accelerated with the coming of independence. People seemed to realize for the first time that modern democratic government was greatly handicapped unless it was based on a literate populace. True, in spite of the comparatively low level of literacy which still prevails largely because of the race against population increase, several general elections have been held, for India has the largest democratic electorate in the world. This great achievement, however, has underlined the necessity of having an electorate basically literate, and therefore more knowledgeable about the issues before the country.

In outlining some of the developments of education in India in the last fifty years, two names may be singled out for the contribution they made—very different in form and content, but one in single-minded devotion to the cause of enlightening their people.

A kindergarten meets outdoors in the tradition of Tagore

A Poet's School

The world-famous poet, Rabindranath Tagore, who composed India's national anthem and won the Nobel Prize, was much interested in the education of children. When he inherited the family estate in rural Bengal, he turned it into a school called *Shantiniketan,* the abode of peace.

The first thing a visitor to Shantiniketan notices is that many of the classes are held out of doors, usually in the shade of the great trees which make the grounds so attractive. This is the way classes were held in ancient India, where many of the teachers lived in the forest, and boys of all ages sought them out and asked for the privilege of being their students. Quite often a boy lived with his teacher as a member of his family and served him in any way he could. If the teacher was in need, the student went out and begged for him.

Tagore realized, for he was a practical man, that modern education cannot always be carried on in the old way, but he felt that much of

116

the old culture had been thoughtlessly abandoned and that smaller classes and a greater freedom and intimacy between the teacher and his students were still possible. One modern innovation was that boys and girls studied together at all stages. Shantiniketan also lays stress on the arts, music, dancing, and drama, with painting and sculpture available for all. Tagore himself was a skilled musician and loved to write songs and plays and to produce them. Sometimes when his students went to Calcutta to make the school better known by presenting a play, Tagore himself was composer, actor, and producer. Tagore's object was to make up for the lack of emotional experience and for the break in India's cultural tradition, which was characteristic of his day, by a school which gave a large measure of joyous freedom.

Eventually Tagore added a university to his educational complex. For many years financing these institutions was a heavy burden on the poet, but now the value of what he did has been recognized, and

The President of India, Dr. S. Radbakrishnan, swears in Indira Gandhi as Minister of Information and Broadcasting

National Physical Laboratory, New Delhi. India has made many contributions in physics

A dormitory providing accommodations for eighty students at the Madras Institute of Technology

Forest Research Institute, Dehradun. Part of the growing National Research Program

financial resources have been provided. Students from abroad often visit Shantiniketan and Vishva Bharati (the university) and spend some time in study there.

Gandhi Plans for Education

Another great Indian, a contemporary of Tagore's, also experimented with education, but he had quite different ideas in mind. This was Gandhi, who in India is often referred to as Mahatma Gandhi, or Gandhiji. What worried Gandhi was that so many children, especially in villages, did not have the opportunity to go to school. Moreover, education for the millions of children in India would cost a great deal if it all had to be paid for out of public funds. How could they have enough useful education at minimum cost? Gandhi's ideas on education were drawn chiefly from modern sources which advocated that education should be combined with manual work. He believed that if this was the general policy, in a short time children would be able to earn all or at least part of their education.

119

Delhi School of Economics. India's planning is based on such research centers

It is not surprising that this idea was difficult to popularize. Many teachers doubted that it could be done and a satisfactory standard of education maintained. The parents objected that if anything was earned by the children it should go to the parents, as after all, it was *their* children who earned the money. Manual labor had not been much respected in the past, and some people felt that it was not compatible with the dignity of education.

But to Gandhi there was something sacred about working with one's hands and making things. Among foreign writers Ruskin and Tolstoy influenced his thinking along these lines. He himself daily spent hours spinning cotton thread which was later woven by handlooms into cloth, the kind of cloth that Gandhi and his closest followers wore exclusively. Jawaharlal Nehru, the great prime minister of India, spun the thread which was later woven into cloth for the wedding dress of his daughter Indira.

Filled with these ideas Gandhi called on experts to help him. A system of primary education was organized under the name of Basic Education, and experimental schools were set up in rural areas. The main body of primary education in India is still of the more conventional type, but the thinking and stimulus of Gandhi have had an effect. As a matter of fact, education in India today is not quite the way either Tagore or Gandhi planned. It is much more like the kind of education found in the schools of America or Europe.

However, the ideas of these two men did help people to wake up and do some thinking about what kind of education was needed, and also how it could be made available for all. The government of India is making steady progress toward the ideal of offering free, compulsory primary education to all children in the country. Since 1960 the aim has been to offer it to children up to eleven years of age, and it is hoped that before many years have passed, children up to fourteen may have the same opportunity. Education is now admitted to be the birthright of every child, and it is just a question of time and resources before the goal is reached. This includes girls as well as boys.

Educational System

India has developed a well-organized educational system which varies somewhat from state to state. It has been developed on three levels, primary, middle, and high school, the whole process usually taking twelve years. Nursery schools are increasingly popular, especially with working mothers.

College Students

The tradition of higher learning and scholarship has always been respected in India, though it has taken new forms to suit the new age. Ancient India had two universities which were famous in other countries, one at Taxila in the north and the other at Nalanda in the east. Eventually they died out. Scholarship persisted but in a less organized way, and it looked back rather then forward. In 1857 the three oldest modern universities in India were opened, in Calcutta, Bombay, and Madras. In recent years many more teaching universities and research institutions have opened their doors. There are now fifty-five universities with over one million students. The ratio of college students to their age group is 1 in 50 in India, 1 in 25 in Britain, and 1 in 5 in the United States. In addition some thousands of Indian students are abroad taking advanced studies.

There is a certain similarity among university students everywhere, an eagerness to explore the universe and especially to follow new branches of learning. There is also manifest an impatience with the past—a restlessness which expresses itself in participation in politics in some countries and social radicalism in others—together with confusion as to aims and directions, especially where the formerly clear-cut objective of political independence has been achieved.

The gulf between the generations is still wide, especially where the parents or grandparents are illiterate. Poverty and its consequent frustration and boredom dog many students who attempt to secure a college education on the proverbial shoestring. A student is particularly bitter when he graduates only to find that the rate of unemployment is a perplexing and depressing factor.

In spite of these problems students as one sees them on the average Indian campus have the gaiety and zest of students everywhere. Many are devoted to games and sports. A few still indulge in the traditional Indian sports of complicated and quite exciting forms of tag known as *hu-tu-tu* and *kabadi*. Indian-style wrestling is taught in gymnasia, usually not on the campus, and is eagerly followed by both academic and non-academic youth. But none of these touches the popularity of cricket, hockey, and soccer. Tennis, badminton, and basketball are also enjoyed.

Many student associations flourish which encourage debating or the arts, and all national holidays and college special days are observed with long and varied "cultural programs," as they are usually called. The conduct of meetings, the committee work required, and the involvement in United Nations observances are all recognized to be excellent training for participation in democratic public affairs. One of the advantages of the extracurricular activities is the opportunity for boys and girls to mingle in a new social atmosphere. High schools usually still separate the sexes, but colleges and professional schools

122

are almost always coeducational, and the opportunities of getting to know one another both in and out of classrooms has done much to enable men and women to work together in public life for furthering national and social interests.

One of the attractive features of Indian students today is their quickly aroused sympathy for the underprivileged. They are sweeping away many of the limitations of caste in the college mess halls and coffee shops, and they are also ready to engage in community service projects in villages or city slums. This may involve hard physical labor such as building an approach road to a village, or it may involve a program for children in the crowded industrial suburbs of a great city.

From this group is coming an altogether new caliber of young government servants who are practical yet enthusiastic and imaginative in tackling the problems of the new community projects which are penetrating into the many thousands of Indian villages.

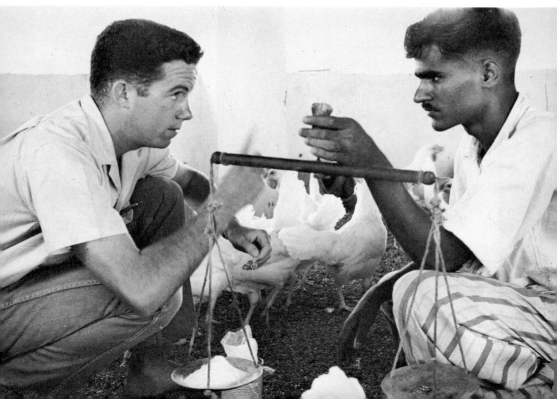

Mohan, the Young Farmer

As Mohan turned off the highway into the side road leading to his father's farm he was startled to hear the *putt-putt* sound of a small engine. Then he saw a group of men gathered around his father, who was proudly looking at the engine that was making the noise.

Mohan had been away for two or three weeks helping his uncle whose farm lay further "in the interior," as the people say. Mohan had, therefore, not heard about the new engine which was evidently the pride and joy of his father's heart. Mohan slid off his bicycle and went forward to look. His father, Dasrath, had attached the engine to the well, and it was pumping water into the irrigation channel.

"And this isn't all it can do," said Dasrath to his neighbors. "It can crush the cane at sugar-making time. It can drive a plow or spray insecticide."

"Have you *seen* it do all this?" asked one of the men suspiciously.

"Indeed I have," replied Dasrath. "It needs some extra attachments, of course, but they are not too difficult to use. It has a five-horsepower motor, but it is not too big or heavy to be carried to any place on the farm where it may be needed."

"What will you do with your oxen?" asked another neighbor.

Mohan reached out his hand and surreptitiously patted one of the animals that stood by. His father looked regretfully at the noble beasts with their strong shoulders and humped backs that had served the family well. Dasrath said slowly, "I don't think I can afford them any-more, whether we grow our own fodder or buy it. Fodder is becoming more and more expensive whichever way you look at it. But we shall miss these old friends, no doubt."

Constructing a mobile pump from war-surplus materials (above). Peace Corps Volunteer and Indian farmer weigh a chicken to check improvement in poultry (left)

125

A Modern Farmer

Mohan was proud of his father whose mind was open to new ideas and methods. Dasrath was the first man in his village to lay aside the old wooden plow of the type that had been used for centuries. He had bought instead a lightweight but strong modern iron plow that did far more than scratch the ground. Now that it would be driven by the new motor instead of drawn by bullocks, cultivation would be deeper and more even, and better crops might be expected. It was his father too who had brought a new kind of fertilizer and improved seed from the government stores, with very good results.

Mohan's father was praised by all for his readiness to explore and adopt progressive ideas. Since Dasrath could read and write, unlike many of his neighbors, he was able to procure and to enjoy many leaflets issued by government agencies to help farmers. He also had in his home a radio which had been made in India, and he enjoyed not only the world and national news which was broadcast but farm news too. The daily or weekly newspaper which came to a few homes had also an important part to play in spreading modern ideas and news. A number of men from the village went to the city every day to deliver milk, and sometimes they visited the movies at the end of their route and brought back ideas they had picked up.

Why Boys Go to Town

The next time the S.E.O. (Social Education Officer) came to the village, Mohan joined the men as they sat and talked with him about the problems of rural India. Naturally there were several points of view. The exodus of young men from the village was causing some distress. They always drifted to the city where many of the boys got jobs in the mills and other places of employment, which they discovered through the National Employment Services or through friends. Those who got regular jobs did well, others lived from hand to mouth, picking up casual jobs, and were no better off than they had been before they left home. A few slipped back to the home village hoping for food and shelter, if not a job.

Transformer brought to a village by oxcart marks the coming of electricity

"There are too many mouths to feed," said one of the men.

But the Social Education Officer said, "It may be so, but there are other ways of looking at it. One is that too many people try to make a living from agriculture, and more should find jobs elsewhere, even if they have to take training. Seventy per cent of the people of India are dependent on the land for their living. Another difficulty is that about three-quarters of all rural households have either no land of their own or less than five acres, which means less than the minimum for self-sustaining farming."

The S.E.O. did not need to go into reasons for the lack of land, for all the people around him knew them well. One was the Hindu system of inheritance. In Britain ancestral land usually passed to the eldest son. In Hindu India the eldest son administered the property after his father's retirement as long as the family stayed together in what is known as a joint family. When, however, a joint family was

127

Bullock carts are frequently seen on country roads

no longer practicable, the land was divided among the sons. In two or three generations the portions became very small, and a man's fields might be separated. This division of land is known as fragmentation.

In recent years a good deal of attention has been paid to finding new land for those who wish to own a small farm and cultivate it for themselves. One method has been to break up large estates. The owners were told that they might keep only as much land as they could cultivate; compensation was given them for the rest, and the government redistributed the land among the landless. In some countries changing the system of holding land has led to revolution, but in India change has taken place in a fair and reasonable manner. Though progress has seemed slow, it has been peaceful and orderly.

Champion of the Landless

Another attempt to equalize land has attracted world-wide attention, and perhaps could happen only in India.

One of Gandhi's followers who was close to him in spirit was Vinoba

128

Bhave. He is now rather elderly but continues his unique service. Vinoba has walked thousands of miles up and down and across his great country. Everywhere he has repeated one message: "Share your land. Give me one-sixth of your land and I will give it to those who have none, for it is a shame that the tillers of the soil should themselves be landless."

When Vinoba comes to a village, he is invariably welcomed with respect. The friends who accompany him on these walking tours set up a simple camp. Word spreads throughout the countryside that he has arrived, and of course his progress along the road has been observed. Crowds come to see him and wait eagerly for him to address them. Vinoba outlines his program and asks for land. "Treat me as a son. Give me my share of your land and I will give it to others." Sometimes his request is received with laughter, but Vinoba is a man

Indian Agricultural Research Institute, New Delhi

of simple dignity and transparent goodness, so his suggestion usually meets with respect and is acted upon. Occasionally, it is true, people want to get cheap credit for generosity, and they donate the least fertile part of their holdings of land. The majority of donors, however, accept the suggestion of Vinoba in his own spirit and give him good and fertile land. In this way many thousands of acres have been donated, and redistribution is gradually taking place.

The question is often asked, "What does Vinoba Bhave actually accomplish by this method which he calls *Bhoodan*, the gift of earth"? Admittedly he has not solved all the problems of the landless; the legislator, the administrator, and the economist still have their tasks to perform, but the climate of opinion has been deeply affected. The element of selfish exploitation fades out of the picture, and the average citizen's social conscience begins to function. Bhave himself has said of his movement, "The main objective is to propagate the right thought by which social and economic maladjustments can be corrected without serious conflict."

Mohan and his friends had seen Vinoba Bhave as he walked through their village, and some of them had joined him and walked in his company until he reached the boundary of the next village.

Mohan felt, however, that there was more to the problem of rural welfare than *Bhoodan* and land reform, and the next time the S.E.O. came to the village, a group of young men plied him with questions. Were there too many people in India? If so, what could be done about it?

The Education Officer did his best to answer.

Population and Food

Undoubtedly India has a large population, the second largest in the world, 439 million by the last census. The density of population varies considerably from 200 per square mile in some areas to 600 per square mile in such areas as the Gangetic plain and in the southernmost tip of India. There is a relationship between food and population. The more crowded areas are the rice-growing areas; rice supports more people per square mile than any other cereal. It is also suited to hot climates. The sorghums and millets are in many places considered to be "the food of the poor." They are, however, very useful cereals and have a wide distribution in both Asia and Africa. "Wheat makes men," but it is most appreciated in temperate climates. Central and north India are excellent wheat-growing areas.

After they had finished discussing food, the young men again began to talk about the growth of population, which has created so many problems.

"Are the families here larger than in other countries?" they inquired.

"No," replied the S.E.O. "Three children per family is quite normal anywhere. What makes the great difference in the growth of population is that more people are living longer."

The boys began to discuss their own village, and they agreed that not nearly so many babies and small children died as formerly, and that there were also more hale and hearty older people around. The

Women transplanting rice to a paddy field in southern Kerala

Central Food Technical Research Institute, Mysore. One of six National Laboratories

expectation of life had doubled in two generations. It was now about forty-six years in India.

"And that means more mouths to feed," said one lad, who was often teased about his hearty appetite.

"Of course it does," said the S.E.O. "but the change has taken place largely because of progress in public health practices. Fewer people die from famine, as better transportation has meant a more equal distribution of basic foodstuffs even though some parts of the country might have a poor harvest."

Many thoughtful citizens are desirous that all the children of India should be "well-born," by which they mean that every child should have adequate opportunities for healthy living and an education. The Family Planning Association of India is one of the social agencies actively spreading these ideas and has considerable help to offer.

The young men of Mohan's village came to the conclusion that the way to solve population and food problems was to learn to produce more food and also more consumer goods. Almost every family represented in the group had one or two members who had gone to join the labor force in the city. Those who remained were considering how they could best modernize their farming. Not only was it important to produce more food for their own needs, but food must also be grown for the hungry city people. It was also important to grow cash crops to add to the prosperity of India among the trading nations of the world.

India is the greatest exporter in the world of peanuts and tea and produces practically all the resinous substance known as *lac*, a component of shellac and many manufactured goods. Rice, jute, raw sugar, spices, and oil seeds are also valuable agricultural exports.

The Cow

Mohan belonged to a Young Farmers' Club which a social worker had helped them organize. One day they went to the city to see three things which would enlarge their horizon: first they visited a newspaper office and press, then they were welcomed at the local station of All India Radio (AIR), and finally they paid a call on a Canadian social worker so that they could really chat with a person from overseas.

Such visits help people not only to get new ideas but to discard old ones. Village people often find it hard to change their traditional attitudes, such as those associated with cows. It is difficult for a non-Hindu to realize how much sentiment is involved in the ancient cult of the veneration of the cow, the origin of which is obscure.

India has one cow to every two people, which means a cow population of over 220 million, the largest cow population in the world. Many cows are useless from the point of view of milk and are turned loose, but where modern dairies are developed, stray cows are no longer seen. When the Aarey Milk Scheme was organized for Greater Bombay with its population of four million people, no fewer than fifteen thousand cows were removed from the streets of Bombay. So great has been the development of Aarey that a milk substation has been opened at Worli with the cooperation of UNICEF and Canada. This milk depot has the largest bottling hall in the world, where ninety thousand bottles of milk are sent out every day.

India is also beginning to manufacture dried milk. The efforts of UNICEF have resulted in a magnificent demonstration of what milk means to the welfare of children and have set a pattern in child care.

Pure drinking water is now available to many village people who had never enjoyed it before. New sanitary wells are not only safer and cleaner but much easier to draw water from—a task which is chiefly performed by women.

Visit to a Tribal Village

Housing is also being transformed. In one village occupied by tribal people the Young Farmers on a visit saw new, neat cottages made of bricks which had been manufactured by tribal people in another village. One of the old type huts had not yet been torn down, and the young men looked at the walls made of small branches or bamboo stems

Making bricks by hand is a rural industry

These sheep may provide wool for the beautiful shawls made in Kashmir

woven together and covered with a mud plaster. The roof was made of sun-baked tiles. The upright posts were slender trees which had been cut and brought in from the jungle, not always quite straight but serviceable. The hut consisted of a single room, which might be called a multipurpose area. There was a storage space for the year's supply of Indian corn, kept in tall jars which had been made by the women. The family slept at one end, and the cattle were accommodated at the other. The people used to say that they did not feel secure about their cattle unless they were near them, as occasionally thieves drove cattle away.

But the new brick cottages were very different from the old huts, as their proud housekeepers pointed out. Each house had four rooms, a kitchen, a storeroom, a family room, and a room for the cattle. In the same village, there was a new maternity home which was a compact

A cowherder in Gujerat, western India

and attractive building. The government usually makes a grant for such institutions of 50 per cent of the cost, the balance being raised by the community. In this case the government had offered to pay 75 per cent to encourage progress among tribal people, but the local community had rejected the extra 25 per cent and paid half the cost of the building. Such sturdy independence is remarkable anywhere.

What Does the Farmer Do?

As in other countries there is considerable variation in the rhythm of a farmer's life. Sometimes he can proceed at a leisurely pace, while at other times he is extremely busy. One of the busy times is shortly before the monsoon rains arrive, usually in June. Some time before the rain is expected, the farmer is busy preparing his fields. In one operation he builds up low-lying areas of a field and puts an embankment of stones and earth around it, rather like a low dike. In this way

136

the precious water will not run off, nor will the equally precious soil be carried away. This process which is known as bunding is hard work, as it is done without machinery, but the farmer knows it is worth while.

Fertilizing is important, as a worn-out field does not give good returns. A natural fertilizer would of course be made from the droppings of the farm animals, but this is the main source of fuel for the family cooking. The women of the family make the droppings into flat cakes which are dried in the sun and then stored for use. (American pioneers who went by oxcart across the treeless prairies also used that type of fuel.) It is probable that Mohan's mother would oppose getting rid of the oxen in favor of a motorized plow, as it would deprive her of a source of fuel.

"These men!" she would say. "An engine is all very well, but how am I to cook their dinner?"

The debate of "fuel versus fertilizer" has been going on for years. In the meantime chemical fertilizers are becoming popular, and they are being developed at a reasonable price by government-sponsored factories. The farmers and their wives are also learning how to make various types of compost, and doing this is often known as women's work.

We have already referred to the improved methods by which Mohan's father did his plowing and harrowing, and to the advantages he found in improved seed. Seeding time often sees the husband and wife working together. The husband guides the plow while the wife pours the seed into the hopper, from which it passes through a hollow bamboo into the furrow. It is a primitive method but fairly efficient.

The pests which are familiar to all farmers are being brought under control with government help, often by aerial spraying. Even the old battle against locusts is being won. In a recent year about 128 locust swarms entered India from the northwest, but as a result of timely and effective control measures, little damage was done to the crops.

India's tremendous program of irrigation and power projects has already been mentioned. These have been made possible in many instances by the cooperation of friendly nations who have lent or given money or contributed personnel and technical skill. India has more than matched the grants-in-aid from her own resources, and Indian engineers and technicians have worked along with their counterparts from all over the world so that a real partnership of sharing has sprung up. Nor has India been lacking in readiness to share her own resources of material or personnel with other countries as opportunity occurs.

Freedom from Hunger

Such an opportunity came through India's membership in the Food and Agricultural Organization (FAO) Committee on Freedom from Hunger. In one campaign India sent a large shipment of sugar to Iran, and Mohan and his friends in the Young Farmers' Club began to think of the people of Iran as neighbors and friends. As a unique contribution India donated a hundred thousand copies of the special postage stamp commemorating the campaign, which were issued on March 21, 1963. Profits from the sale of these stamps to collectors went to buy food for Iran.

Cow-dung cakes used for fuel are for sale

A Saora woman picks rice seedlings for transplanting. Her baby spends the day in a cloth pack

Another helpful effort in which India is giving full cooperation is the Mysore Project for food preservation. The project operates an institute in Mysore, south India, where under the leadership of the FAO, training is given to people from various countries in South Asia facing similar problems. The wastage of food in the past has been enormous, sometimes from the depredations of birds and wild beasts who feed on the crops in the fields, and sometimes from rats who get into the storage centers in the towns. There is also the glut on the market which occurs when the season is at its height, as for tomatoes, mangoes, or oranges. Indian housekeepers are skilled in the arts of making pickles and chutneys and dehydrating vegetables, but like the women of other countries they now call on the resources of modern scientific food preservation to cope with the twin problems of wasted food and subnourished people. Indians have been famous for their hospitality, and

139

Camel carts near Delhi

among those who can afford it, much is done in the way of feeding the poor; but Mohan and his friends have begun to realize that the distribution of food is not an individual matter but an important national and international problem which all must help to solve.

We must not think, however, that all Mohan's life is spent in hard work and solving problems. Children everywhere have their games, and the young men have their favorite sports, such as wrestling and the complicated forms of tag that Indian youths enjoy. Singing parties, folk dancing and the drama, the old-fashioned ballad singer, and the storytellers who still wander from village to village are part of the traditional village life. On a larger scale, weddings, festivals, and pilgrimages add movement and color.

Here is part of a folk song sung by peasant women of Rajasthan:

> The rains have begun in June, and the millet sowing too,
> My mother is bringing my lunch to the field.
>   Praise God, praise.

In the month of July the millet grew and the weeding began,
But the creeping vines of the small gourds are not disturbed.
  Praise God, praise.

In August there will be peanuts and also lentils,
We shall eat millet bread.
  Praise God, praise.

In September there are hopes of a good crop, and the
  watchers are crying to scare away the birds;
We shall live day and night in the fields.
  Praise God, praise.

In October will come maize, eat as many cobs as you like.
Thou didst make the maize in October.
  Praise God, praise.

In November will come the season of the moneylender,
  to settle the account,
After giving and taking we shall be free.
  Praise God, praise.

In December it will be cold, and our skins will be chapped;
What if our skin *is* chapped?
  Praise God, praise.

Bhakra Nangal Dam on the Sutlej River

Surjit Interprets Industry

When Surjit came home for a visit in Gopalpur, he urged Jim and Ted to come to the city and let him show them around the industrial areas. Since he was employed by the Indian National Trade Union (INTUC), he would be a suitable and helpful interpreter of the way of life led by men and women in the ranks of labor.

Ted and Jim were again very fortunate in having Indian hospitality extended to them during their stay in the city. Surjit himself had only a small bachelor apartment, but he introduced them to Sivaram and Kamala, friends of his, and they cordially invited the boys to stay with them.

Sivaram was the editor of an important newspaper, the *Samachar* (News), which was owned by the Trade Union. The press and editorial offices were in a wing of a large, handsome building known as Union House. It was surrounded by wide lawns and a well-laid-out garden. The boys saw how much the garden was appreciated. Sometimes a committee of workers from one of the nearby mills would sit on the lawn to conduct a meeting; sometimes a solitary young man in a quiet corner would be lost in a book.

In the main part of the building were a large auditorium, an excellent library, Union offices, several consulting rooms, and three or four class-rooms for adult education. In another part of the building were two or three apartments, in one of which lived Sivaram and his charming wife, Kamala. Kamala was a college graduate, always keen and ready to discuss labor affairs with her husband and his friends, but she was also much involved in household matters as the house was frequently overflowing with guests, and she had three small children to look after.

"But wait, just wait," said Kamala. "As soon as the children are big, I will be an active worker again, as I was before I was married."

Kanji—Labor Leader

It was in Sivaram's home that the boys met Kanji, the veteran labor leader whom everyone treated with respect and affection. Kanji began to talk to Ted and Jim about his varied experience.

"When were you first interested in labor?" they asked.

Kanji's eyes twinkled. "A little boy of six was promised that he would see a miracle," he said. "That evening he went with his parents to a cotton mill in Parel, a suburb of Bombay. There at half-past six some-one—could it have been his mother?—pressed a button and the whole mill shone with electric light."

"When was that?" asked Jim.

"More than sixty years ago," Kanji replied, "and that was when my interest in mills and mill people began, which has been the main interest of my life."

"If you'll excuse me for saying so, sir," said Ted, "I understand that your family did not always share your interest."

"No, naturally it took them some time to come around to my point of view," replied Kanji, "because you see my father owned and managed a mill. He was accustomed to looking at things from one point of view— profits. He was not an unkind man, but he knew very little about how his employees lived or what their problems were. Actually, he should be praised more than blamed, because it took courage to invest in modern industry in those days. You see, there had to be a great change in Indian thinking before people were willing to invest."

"What sort of change?" asked Jim.

Capital and Labor

"Oh, for one thing, in concepts of saving and investment. Why do you save and how do *you* do it?"

Jim replied, "Well, to begin with, I spend less for a while so that I can accumulate enough money to do something special with it. If the money is put in a bank, it will earn interest."

"Very good, and when a fair amount has been saved, what do you do then?"

144

Sindri Fertilizer Plant, Madhya Pradesh State

"Either I buy something I have been saving for, such as a camera, or I might buy government bonds, or invest in something that pays better interest. After some time I shall have some capital to use in starting a business."

Kanji said, "Yes, I understand, but all this seemed quite strange to many people when I was a boy. If a man wanted to save, there were only two or three ways in which he could do it. One was to buy jewelry for his wife."

The boys exclaimed in surprise, but Kanji smiled and went on, "It was really a good idea, because if a man got heavily into debt, his wife's jewelry could not be seized by the creditors. Many a woman was a walking savings bank. If she and her husband needed some ready cash, she could sell a piece of jewelry.

"A man could also buy real estate, or purchase gold and hide it until it was needed—I say 'hide it' because there were no banks in which to deposit it."

"That suggests a much less secure and orderly society than India now has," said Ted.

"That was true at one time," said Kanji, "but when the British established a government of law and order they started railways, banks, and industries. Since Indians were at first very reluctant to invest capital in such enterprises, shares were at first owned chiefly by British investors. The idea of putting one's savings to productive use through the accumulation and investment of capital gradually became accepted and practiced. At first the idea of investing in such novel enterprises as cotton mills or railways seemed very risky indeed, but after a while adventurous men did invest, and increasingly individuals and firms put capital into such things as factories, railways, and mines, and were pleased with the results."

"It involved a great change in thinking, as you pointed out, Kanji. Did everything go smoothly?" asked Jim.

Howrah Bridge across the Hoaghly River, Calcutta

"Much better than you might expect," said Kanji, "but two things still had to be learned. Some mill owners became excited about quick returns on their investment and used the machinery ruthlessly, with the result that soon there were mechanical breakdowns. The other temptation was to use workers in the same way they used the machines, push them to the limit."

"But that was not peculiar to India," said Ted. "Other countries too have had to learn that long hours, poor conditions, and child labor could not be tolerated, and were unnecessary."

Kanji agreed and said, "There were various social movements in the world which helped to improve conditions, but one of the most important, both in India and the West, was the rise of labor unions. Indian labor unions were encouraged by unions in Britain. The first union in India was organized in 1918, and a few years later India became a member of the International Labor Organization (I.L.O.) in Geneva."

"Where did the Indian unions find their leadership?" asked Ted.

"Just where the British unions found theirs, not only in the ranks of labor itself, but also among young university graduates who were keenly interested in the labor unions and were willing to work for the movement both in the unions and in government bodies at different levels."

Developing Industries

"When did all this development of industry take place?" asked Jim. "Was the cotton mill you told us about one of the first?"

"Oh no," said Kanji, "there were some much older than that. Modern industry in India began in the decade 1850 to 1860, mostly in the Calcutta and Bombay areas. In Calcutta there were jute mills as well as cotton, as jute is virtually an Indian monopoly; but cotton was the first big business. Cotton was developed chiefly with Indian capital and enterprise; jute with foreign initiative. Coal mining was also being developed, and this was of great importance in providing power for the mills. It was also the fuel for the newly organized railways which were

Bombay traffic consists of trolleys, buses, private cars, and even bullock carts

bringing raw materials to the mills and distributing the finished product. Oil and electric engines came much later."

"With all this industrial development what happened to the industrial workers?" asked Ted. "I'm sure you were much interested in them."

"Fortunately," said Kanji, "a social conscience began to develop in both India and England. In India social legislation was enacted from time to time. The first Factory Act was passed in 1881, and it has been revised a number of times to bring it up to date. Things moved slowly at first, but a great change has taken place. There is now no child labor in the mills. Women are not allowed to work on the night shift. Instead of extremely long hours the mills now have three shifts a day, each one with a lunch break. Some of the mills have excellent cafeterias, or as we call them, canteens. Women are allowed time off with pay when a baby is born, and there are good day nurseries, or crèches, to take care of small children while their mothers are working. There is workmen's compensation to take care of men and women who are injured on the job. There are a number of fringe benefits which I won't take the time to mention just now. Things are indeed much better than in the bad old days when we worked by trial and error."

"Are there many women workers employed in factories?" asked Ted.

"Not so many as men, but Indian women of the lower income groups are willing workers. Moreover they are considered more skillful than men in some departments, such as the spinning operations of a cotton mill." Kanji then said, "You have a good friend with you," indicating Surjit. "I have known him for years, and I don't think you could have a better guide. I hope he will find time to show you around the mills and labor settlements."

"Thank you, sir, we shall be glad of Surjit's help. And thank you too for telling us such interesting things."

"You are indeed welcome," said Kanji, bidding them farewell with folded hands in the Indian manner.

Villagers in the Mills

Next day the three young men began their tour by going through a cotton mill. Aside from all the processes they saw, the boys were

Labor leaders confer with the Minister of Labor for Madhya Pradesh State

especially interested in looking at the personnel. Later they remarked to Surjit, "These people working in the mills look very much like the people we saw in Chandra's village, and some other villages we have visited."

"Of course they do," replied Surjit, "because that is where most of them come from. You know how hard it is to find jobs in a village, so some of the young men like myself leave home to see if we can do better. It is not difficult for a chap like me who has had some education to settle down in a town, but it is a great change for a man who is a real villager. The sanitation of a town, for example, is very different from the sanitation of a village. There is probably no well in the town, only a water tap for which a number of people compete. There are crowds everywhere; a man can never be alone, yet he may be very lonely. The shops are full of exciting things to buy, and a week's wages soon disappear in spite of resolutions about sending home money to help the family. But there is excitement about town life, and people seldom return to the village to stay."

"Do they often go back to visit?"

Workers test radios at Bharat Electronics, Bangalore

Bhilai Blast Furnace in Madhya Pradesh State

"Yes, indeed, in the early days of mill labor this was a great botheration to the employers, and there was a good deal of talk about 'absenteeism.' When harvest time came, many of the men went back to the village to help with the crops. If a man heard that one of his relations was getting married, of course he went off to enjoy the wedding! The mill management complained that the labor force was very unstable and that the turnover was too high. Fortunately, things have improved, and more men are working steadily and consequently are earning more."

"How did the improvement take place?"

"Oh, there were a number of factors. One was the development of better housing so that a man could have his wife and children with him. But there is still a great deal to be accomplished in this respect as you will see tomorrow when I show you the old and new style of housing

151

for the labor force. I may mention some of the fringe benefits: medical services are readily available, and education is within the reach of both children and adults."

"Haven't the mills changed too?"

"Certainly they have, and there is real ambition on the part of industry to keep India among the important industrial nations of the world. Do you remember telling me the other day how surprised you were in reading Indian history recently to find that for a long time India was a rich exporting country, and there was little the West had to offer that she wanted? But things are different now. There are a great many things that the West offers that Indians would like to have, but they are learning that they must make many of these goods themselves, and that is just what is happening—cars, sewing machines, railway engines, radios, and many more.

"India is also exporting more manufactured goods to other nations as well as the traditional raw material. To take an example at random, in 1963 one Indian firm sold 75,000 pairs of footwear to Italy and 100,000 pairs to West Germany."

"Let us hope that someday we shall have a really cooperative world economy," said Ted.

The next day was a holiday, and Surjit said that he was free to start the tour of the industrial living areas that Ted and Jim had been so eager to see.

A "Slum" Area

They went first to a district where some thousands of people lived who were employed in mills. In the early days of the mills when men came to the city looking for work, they were anxious to find someplace to which they could bring their wives and children, but the few tenement houses that had been built by the mills were crowded and dreary places. The village men could not find any accommodation at all, good, bad, or indifferent, as the days went by.

On the edge of the city, however, within walking distance of the mill area there was vacant land. A small group of men who knew each other

152

decided that they could do something there, so they became squatters: in other words they camped out on the land. Eventually, it is true, they found that they had to pay ground rent to the owner, but it was a small sum they could afford. The men then proceeded to make their huts, literally of bits and pieces. By hunting around they discovered scraps of wood, some tin sheeting, old cans that could be hammered flat, and of course they knew how to handle earth to make walls and floors as they had done in the village. The huts were built without reference to any overall plan with the result that the lanes between the houses were crooked and narrow. There were no services at all as the settlement was outside the city limits. Thus there was no provision for sanitation or street lighting, nor was there any water supply except for two or three wells which had been dug when the area was farm land. The situation would have seemed hopeless to many people, but these pioneers accepted it with courage and even with cheerfulness. In the course of time many people improved their huts in various ways and made them both more permanent and more attractive. Some of the occupants had artistic ability, and they would whitewash a wall and paint on it a colorful design or a mural. Some of them organized a small elementary school for the children. A veranda or even a shady tree was used for the classroom; the children sat on the ground and wrote on slates. The teacher was a young man, maybe a college student, who was paid cooperatively. The men in the settlement organized themselves into wards, each with a ward committee; when later they found opportunities for improving affairs, they knew how to talk things over in a democratic way and make group decisions. Eventually the municipality took over the district and made some improvements in public services but then proceeded to charge taxes, which did not suit the happy-go-lucky spirit of the original settlers at all!

If Ted and Jim had not had Surjit with them to interpret what they saw, the boys would have been much depressed by the sight of so many people living under what seemed "slum" conditions. All the residents, however, were cheerful and friendly. They did indeed hope for better days ahead, chiefly for the sake of the children, but in the meantime they were doing the best they could.

Labor Union Services

When they had finished their tour of this area, Surjit thought it was time to cheer up his friends, and said, "Let's go and have lunch."

Instead of the response he expected, Jim and Ted looked quite alarmed and said, "But where?"

"Not here," said Surjit quickly. "I'm sure you'll like the place we are going to now."

In a few minutes they were entering a large four-story building, where on the ground floor there was a clean and attractive cafeteria. They found a table and enjoyed a delicious lunch.

"Who runs this place?" asked Jim.

"A committee of women," said Surjit, "wives of men who work in the mills and are members of the union. Most of the people who eat here are men, as you see, but the planning and supervision are done by the women's branch of the union—the whole building, of course, belongs to the union. Would you like to see some of the other activities?"

New Secretariat Building, Government of West Bengal, Calcutta

International Conference of Social Work meets at the Trade Union Center, Indore

They found that a variety of projects were carried on there. On the ground floor near the cafeteria was a shop for grain and staple groceries where things were sold at discount prices. Upstairs was a large room for women's activities where a number of women were cutting out or sewing garments needed by their families. Some of them had learned how to use a sewing machine, and they would return from time to time and rent a machine by the hour for a small sum. There was also a library in an adjoining room which the women seemed to appreciate.

"Can many women read?" Ted inquired.

"Many more are learning now than a few years ago. If you come to this window, you can see an attractive building a little way off. Yes, that's the one you're pointing at. That is the Women's Club House where many activities and social affairs are carried on, and learning to read is one of them. The women teach one another."

Tata Iron and Steel Plant, Jamshedpur in eastern India

"Where do the men learn?"

"We'll discover that next," said Surjit, and led the way to a neighboring building. On the ground floor was the office of the Workers' Educational Organization. There Jim and Ted were given a great deal of interesting information and some literature before going upstairs to see a class in action. They found about thirty men taking part in a lively discussion. They were all participants in a three months' training course to become worker-teachers. All of them earned their living in industry, but the group at the W.E.O. were better educated than most of the other workers, and they were therefore glad of the opportunity of learning how to teach and how to interest people in further education. The course would conclude with a ten days' tour of some of the important places in India. The group would visit historical places and such modern developments as one of the big HYDEL projects. The Workers' Education program was jointly sponsored by the management of the local mills, the trade union, and a special branch of the Ministry of Education, Government of India.

When the class in session heard who Ted and Jim were, the boys were cordially welcomed and asked to make speeches. Jim suggested, however, that they would be glad to answer questions, and they spent the next half-hour answering a brisk volley of questions about the countries they had come from and especially about the conditions of labor and industry there. Very much impressed by what they had heard and seen, the three young men continued their tour.

Nearby was another large building, a hospital for women and children. The boys were invited to see some of the offices and service areas, and they were impressed by the cleanliness and efficiency they saw.

As they walked down the road to their next point of call, they met an elderly man who greeted them cordially; his name was Ram Singh and he proved to be a remarkable man as Surjit told them his story later. He came from a very poor family and had little opportunity for education. He had, however, a great deal of natural ability, and he had risen through the labor movement to a position of responsibility and leadership. In fact, for several years he had been elected to the State Legislative Assembly. Ram Singh was pleased to hear the compliments of Jim and Ted on what they had seen, but he was full of plans for the future. Before letting them go further, he took them to the top of one of the high buildings where they could get a panoramic view, and he showed them the site where the new sports stadium was going to be built very soon. After they had parted from Ram Singh, they had another surprise.

Just in front of them was a line of little children accompanied by two pretty young teachers.

"Where are they going?" asked Ted.

"Let's follow and see," said Surjit.

The children led them to a charming park where everything was scaled to sizes comfortable for children. The park was well supplied with the usual playground equipment, but in addition it had a wading pool and an open-air theater; on one side was a large contour map of India made in cement.

But time was passing, and after a few words with the teachers, Surjit tactfully drew them away. "There is one thing more you must see, and perhaps it is the most important of all."

When the boys looked puzzled, he reminded them of the unplanned housing area that had so much depressed them when they had visited it in the morning, and said, "Now to end the day I want to show you something that will cheer you up."

New Housing for Workers

While the boys were trying to guess what he meant, Surjit led them down the street and around a corner into a housing area they had not seen before. The houses were all one-family cottages, well-built and modern. Each house had its own garden of shrubs and flowers, and some had a vegetable patch also. Surjit walked up the path to one of the houses and was met by a smiling man who cordially invited them to come in. Surjit introduced Ted and Jim and said, "These young men would appreciate visiting your home, Hari, if you and your wife don't mind. You see the houses and way of living here are very different from those in their own countries."

"Come in, come in and welcome. See anything you like. Look, wife, here are two young men from overseas."

Hari's wife, Tara, looked up cheerfully from the low fireplace in front of which she was sitting and cooking the evening meal. She was about to stand up to greet them, but they begged her not to disturb herself. They noticed that unlike the village women they had seen, Tara was using charcoal for fuel, and she also had a small kerosene oil stove on which she could boil water quickly. When the boys began to look around the house, she put on the kettle.

Ted and Jim saw that the house had a small courtyard with a porch on one side. There was a bathing place at the back and to one side a storeroom and two bedrooms. In the front of the house was a living room with a small table and two or three chairs. There was also a small cotton rug on the floor for those who did not care to sit on chairs—"perched up" as they would have said. In the bedrooms the bedsteads had wooden frames laced across with wide tape or cord. Some pegs on the wall had garments hanging on them, but other things were kept in one or two small metal trunks. For pictures there were framed family photographs and a colored print of a religious subject.

The most attractive place in the house was the kitchen with its shining brass utensils neatly arranged. There the family usually ate. By this time Tara had tea ready for her guests, sweet, hot and milky. With it she served some sweets she had made that morning, a few salty biscuits that had been bought at the store, and bananas. It seemed a long time since the boys had had their lunch so they appreciated Tara's hospitality. She was eager to ask questions about their mothers and their home life, and the boys began to feel that there was much they had in common with this friendly family.

South Indian temple at Bhuvaneswar

160

India's Heritage of Beauty

The Museum of Modern Art in New York is in two sections: in one there are paintings and sculptures which may be described as abstract or subjective. Many visitors find this section puzzling. Is art primarily self-expression or is it a means of communication? Such questions as to the philosophy of art come to the mind of a visitor to this gallery.

In the other section, however, things are different. It contains exhibits of many articles of contemporary design for use in the home or in industry. Some of these things have been handcrafted and others produced by machinery.

At one time articles designed for domestic use were rather elaborately decorated, perhaps in an effort to make one's daily work more attractive: keys in the Middle Ages, for example, and stoves in the nineteenth century. Some old furniture was sturdily built and useful but too ornate in design to suit present tastes. Now, however, the smooth, flowing lines of modern design are beautiful and satisfying to us, and things are functionally much more useful than previous articles of the same category.

The question naturally arises, Which section of the Museum more adequately interprets and expresses the soul of the American people of this generation?—a difficult question to answer.

Similar questions may be asked by young people in India today. They are surrounded by art treasures of the past which are today more praised and studied than ever before. Many of these are rich with decorative detail and symbolism. Along with these, in the heritage from the past, is the persistence of handmade articles in daily use which have their own beauty and are beginning to meet with new appreciation. And—to note a new development—there are now on the market many articles, made in India, new in use or in design. Which form of art most adequately expresses the meaning of life to the young adult today? All have elements of value which should not be discarded: how can a selective process bring them into harmony and progress?

Hindu art, especially in sculpture and painting, has traditionally manifested an exuberant and lavish use of detail that tends to stun the unaccustomed observer. Was it perhaps inspired by the exuberance of nature at certain seasons? The density of the tropical jungle; the seed dropped by a bird which against all odds grows into a tree and splits the wall of a building; the rush of growth and the transformation of the face of nature when the monsoon breaks; the fertility of man and beast which is constantly emphasized in rituals—all these must have played their part.

Outside influences, however, sometimes impose a more restrained pattern. The sculpture of the Kushans (first century A.D.) had lean, spare lines that suggested the austerity of the desert. This influence reappeared with Islamic architecture, though sculpture was not part of their art. One may see it again today in the modern architecture of buildings in the major Indian cities, and most of all in Chandigarh, the new capital of the Punjab.

Architecture

A survey of the arts and crafts of India, however brief, may well begin with architecture. Except for the remains of the Indus Valley civilization, not many ancient buildings have survived. Probably this is because they were for a long time made of wood, a perishable material especially in the Indian climate. In the early stages of Buddhist cave temples the roofs were carefully carved into a semblance of wooden beams and supports. In one such cave the bottoms of the upright columns are represented as standing in ceramic containers, because the early wooden pillars were thus protected from termites.

In Europe, Gothic architecture was inspired by trees in the forest. In India, shrines were made by bending the boughs of trees and tying

Mogul architecture at Agra is a typical example of Islamic influence

them to upright posts. This method of contriving a building, whether for religious or domestic use, was developed into the curved roofs seen in some places today, and especially into the curvilinear towers of one style of Hindu temple. (Other styles had wedge-shaped or star-shaped towers.)

The material of buildings naturally depends on local resources. The Indus Valley culture used brick and tile, materials which are still extensively used where the local clay is suitable. Elsewhere villages continue to be made of earth given cohesion by a mixture of cow dung and straw. In modern buildings, of course, materials such as steel, aluminum, concrete, and glass are used, which need not be local products.

Town-planning, Old and New

The concept of a planned city was not new to India. There have been three of note.

The first was Fatehpur-Sikri built by Akbar, the Grand Mogul, who has also been called the Prince of Dreamers. He daringly combined Hindu and Islamic elements of style and chose as his material the local red sandstone, which in combination with white marble became the hallmark of Mogul builders. It has been said that the city of Fatehpur-Sikri "filled the eyes of youth forever afterwards with the courage of dreams."

The next planned city was Jaipur, which was built by the Rajput king Jai Singh in the eighteenth century. Fatehpur has long since been deserted and is now only a place of call for travelers, but Jaipur is still a bustling city, whose wide streets—planned before the days of motorcars—give it a surprisingly modern look. Jai Singh is said to have "combined the commercial interests of Marwar with the poetry of the stars." In other words, he recognized that the prosperity of the city would depend in no small measure on the well-organized district market (*mandi*) which still flourishes. The stars were studied in an observatory which is said to be remarkably accurate.

The third city is, of course, Chandigarh, an outstanding example of modern town planning and architectural development along new lines. In the partition that followed independence, part of the Punjab and the old state capital went over to Pakistan. A new capital was inevitable. The site of Chandigarh was chosen with great care, and the architects who were invited to design and develop it were an international team both sensitive and competent. The leader was the famous Le Corbusier, with his inspiring personality. An Indian writer describes him:

"Having started as a painter and having groped his way towards the mother of all arts, architecture, he had the necessary empathy to sense the direction of Indian genius for the future. And the tackling of thousands of complicated and difficult problems, of clearing a jungle while preserving the beautiful groves of trees,

Carvings on one of the great Shore Temples

of creating a lake to mirror the nearby mountains, . . . of revealing the texture of local stone, of researching in new materials and perfecting them for the future, above all to build an inspired poetic capital for a modern government, embodying the ideals of humanity, justice and efficiency, is certainly a formidable achievement."

So there stands Chandigarh, a dream city come true, on the wide wheat-bearing plain of the Punjab with the Himalaya Mountains blue in the background.

In building a city which was to be primarily a seat of government, in which industry would not occupy a dominant position, attention was given chiefly to buildings for the administration and houses in which many different categories of workers would live, each one with comfort and dignity. There are some who think that the achievement of housing along modern lines was the more remarkable achievement of the two. In this connection it has been remarked that Le Corbusier "has indeed carried out a revolution. . . . If he could not get over the class system, (which) divided the rich from the poor, all the same he released a social revolution in the lives of the poor by giving them verandas, smokeless kitchens, flush lavatories, front gardens, and the urge to demand a classless and casteless society."

Closely connected with architecture in India is sculpture in stone; indeed in India there is an intimacy between architecture and sculpture which probably occurs nowhere else.

A Westerner tends to think of architecture as being concerned primarily with space. A given quantity of space is needed or available: how then can it be contained and used? There are some Hindu buildings which do use this concept as a Western builder would, but not infrequently the concept has been that of *mass* to be molded and formed as sculpture is shaped. Islamic architecture has space value because the mosque is a place of congregational worship; so also is a Buddhist temple or a Christian church. In the Hindu temple the

Ellora Rock Temple, hewn—not built—from solid rock

166

Carvings in the Elephanta Caves, Bombay

heart of the building is the cell which is the inner sanctum. Into it the worshipper advances alone.

The outstanding example of the combination of architecture and sculpture is the temple at Ellora (seventh century A.D.), which was not built, but created by being carved out of the living rock. The innumerable sculptures with which it is covered are an integral part of the whole. This is one of the great combined achievements of architecture and sculpture in the world.

Sculpture

The earliest sculpture found in India is that of the Indus Valley civilization. Two examples have become well known. One is a small

168

figure, seven inches high, of the upper part of the body of a man of dignity, which has been carved from limestone. The other is a charming bronze figure of a dancing girl. Well known also are the carved seals which are both numerous and well done. These seals have inscriptions in the as yet undeciphered pictographic script and many representations of animals incised with clear, effective lines.

Early Buddhist sculpture. Buddha was represented by symbols, not as a person

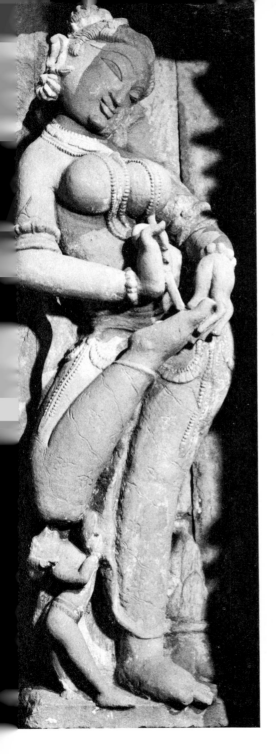

Statue of a woman removing a thorn from her foot

Buddha delivering first sermon, Sarnath Museum

Dancing goddess, Behn Temple, Mysore

A long interval of some centuries elapsed before the new life generated by Buddhism flowered into art. The earliest Buddhist sculptures did not represent their founder in person, but preferred to use a symbol of Buddha, such as the Bo Tree or the Wheel of the Law. Later the expansion and influence of the Roman Empire, which was accompanied by the diffusion of Greek culture even beyond the confines of Roman law, had an effect in north India and elsewhere, and Buddhist art came into its own. In the courts of the kings of northwest India developed a type of art known as Gandharan, which shows a strong Greek influence. Images of Buddha began to appear, not only in north India, but in Central and Eastern Asia and further south in Cambodia and Java.

Hindu art was naturally stimulated by the development of Buddhist and Jain sculpture, and sometimes there were interesting blends of the two strains, as when fertility deities appear in the Buddhist setting.

The Mauryan period (about 300 to 200 B.C.) had three developments of sculpture: the art of the court, the simple art cult of the forest, and in between a development of terra-cotta art which was produced by artists of skill but with less formality than was displayed by the court artists. A charming recurring theme of that period represents a woman leaning against a tree, for the saying is that "the touch of a beautiful woman's foot will bring a tree into flower."

Much of what has been written about sculpture in stone or stucco or terra-cotta is applicable also to the fine work in bronze for which south India in particular is justly renowned. The bronze figure of the dancing girl which is part of the legacy of the Indus Valley civilization was followed by bronzes in south India which have been famous since very ancient times. Many were exported to Nepal, Tibet, and the countries of Southeast Asia. With the spread of Buddhism went figures of bronze as well as of stone, and these deeply influenced the countries of the East to which the religion was carried. Most of the Indian bronzes were made by the *cire perdue* method, in which the figure was first modeled in wax and the wax then covered with clay. When heat was applied, the wax melted and ran out, and the hollow mold was then filled with molten metal. It is said that the south Indian school of bronze casters has not been excelled in the world.

In looking at Indian sculpture of any period or milieu there are certain common characteristics.

One is the sense of rhythmic action. In almost every sculptured figure there will be a bent knee or a hip movement or a gesture of the hands (*mudra*). There is often too a sense of a deep indrawn breath, such as a dancer might draw when reaching the climactic moment.

One has only to attempt a description of sculpture to realize that Indian art has passed imperceptibly from architecture to sculpture and into the dance. The dance and sculpture in India have been inextricably combined. Probably no sculptors are more skilled in depicting the varied rhythms of motion than are those of India. It is by discover-

172

ing the rhythm that a non-Indian can find a clue to appreciation, even of the multiple-limbed Hindu images which tend to distract and puzzle the uninitiated observer. The explanation that is generally offered is that by adding limbs the impression of a superperson is created. But it is more helpful to think of the figure as being in a dance pose and thereby begin to perceive the lovely rhythm that reveals the creative spirit of the sculptor.

Painting

India has some primitive rock paintings comparable with those found elsewhere, but not many have been discovered nor have they been intensively studied.

One of her greatest achievements in painting—as in sculpture— are the pictures found on the walls of cave temples. Found in the same escarpment in western India are the caves which developed chiefly sculpture, such as those at Ellora, and the caves where the decoration is painting, such as Ajanta. Both complexes of caves were developed about the fourth to the seventh centuries, in gradual sequence. The religious motif is predominantly Buddhist, though Jain and Hindu elements are also found.

For many centuries after the decline of Buddhism, the cave temples were not only unused but neglected to such an extent that they were overgrown with jungle. They were rediscovered by accident and were restored. They are now considered part of India's national treasures and have won world-wide attention.

We do not know how paintings were produced on cave walls, as the lighting was poor, but it is supposed that mirrors were used to reflect light into dark corners. The artists were employed by the monks of the various monasteries who used the caves for their living quarters and their chapels, and it is remarkable to what extent the paintings reflect a *joie de vivre,* which is not generally regarded as monastic, and also a minute and delighted observation of nature and of people in the world outside. It has been remarked that "here we see the whole life of ancient India in panorama."

173

Mural painting spread from the walls of the caves into the outside world to adorn temples and palaces. It went even further: as Indian cultural influences spread in Central Asia, the art of mural painting went too, and we find traces of a great tide of art from Afghanistan and Chinese Turkestan on the west along the ancient caravan trade routes such as the "Silk Road." The dry sands and air of Central Asia have preserved many of these treasures, which have only recently been rediscovered through the efforts of such noted explorers as Sir Aurel Stein. Individual though Chinese art is, and not to be mistaken for any other, those who know Indian art can see its influence even in China.

The Miniatures

A further development of Indian art took place in Bengal (about 750 to 1200) but with a new medium—palm leaves. For centuries palm leaves were the material from which books were made. They were cut in uniform, long, narrow strips, and one or two holes were

Examples of folk art from murals on the walls of village cottages

174

Painting of a tribal dance of warriors

punched in each leaf (as is done in loose-leaf notebooks today). Then the leaves were threaded on cords. Of course the leaves were brittle and fragile, and considerable care had to be taken to preserve them, but many thousands of them survived in libraries and were studied and prized by scholars.

Just as in Europe manuscripts were copied and illumined by hand, in India the palm-leaf manuscripts were made. From this time on Indian art falls into two main categories, the murals and the "miniatures." Unfortunately, the word "miniature" does not convey quite the full meaning to people of today. We think of a miniature as being very small. Actually it was an illustration of a book and might be either very small or of considerable size, only, of course, it was small compared with a mural. The word "miniature" comes from the verb *miniat* which means "to paint with vermillion" (*minium* or red lead). An alternative to painting on manuscript was to paint on specially prepared boards.

The Pala and Sena dynasties of Bengal developed much nonmural art, and as they were in touch with trans-Asian caravan routes, they shared in the distribution of Indian painting.

175

After 1400, paper was used for manuscripts, and it was at first carefully cut to resemble palm leaves—just as the earliest stone architecture simulated wood when possible. The use of paper was much regretted by some artists and scholars, but it certainly made possible a wider diffusion of art and a longer life for manuscripts.

The subjects of these early paintings were usually religious, but other subjects crept in, though quite often a secular theme was given a religious value by treating it symbolically—as has been done elsewhere. The life of Buddha and the Jataka tales were favorites.

The two great schools of miniature painting are the Rajput and the Mogul. Both were known as miniature because they were developed as illustrations for manuscripts rather than as murals.

Rajput painting flourished in the seventeenth and eighteenth centuries in the region of north central India which is now known as Rajastan. The themes of the Rajput painters were drawn from the epics and romances, themes of love or religion, and also visual interpretations of musical modes. Times and seasons are sensitively interpreted in Indian music; for example, the music played at midnight would be quite different from music played in the morning or afternoon. The artists undertook to show these fine nuances in line and color.

The Moguls were forbidden by their religion to have "graven images," but there was a strong trend toward pleasure in color and line, especially emanating from Persia. During the conflict of Islamic and Hindu forces following the retreat of Buddhism, there was a deterioration in art, except for the folk art which has persisted through the centuries undeterred by any political upheavals. As the country became more settled politically, the Moguls made their contribution not only to architecture as we have seen but to painting. They imported court painters and set up ateliers for their use. Hindu artists and craftsmen were also welcomed and encouraged.

Sources of Inspiration

With the decline of Mogul power and subsequent unrest and change of government, for a time the arts did not flourish, except in the courts of the princely rulers. With the new, independent government, however, very definite encouragement has been given to artists to express themselves, especially in the media of modern art and communication. The government Ministry of Cultural Affairs has organized several *Akademi* (academies) to encourage and assist writers, musicians, painters, and sculptors, and Indians have responded quickly and with enthusiasm to the new opportunities of expressing ancient skills and deep emotions. The cinema is one of these new expressions which has been taken up with enthusiasm. India now has the second largest film industry in the world.

Just as Indian sculpture expresses dynamic emotions and activity, so we find the same spirit in painting. Rembrandt is said to have admired the skill of Mogul artists in drawing, and the vitality of line which is characteristic of Indian folk art is carried over into the more

Mask of a wicked king from a classical dance

refined ways of expression. At the same time there is an abiding link between folk art and the more classical or disciplined methods of expression. It is said that the Rajput miniature owes its origin to the rise of vernacular literature and the introduction of paper. (A comparison might well be made with the development of the arts in Europe —the use of the basic language and the printing press.)

The Rajput school tended to think symbolically and the Mogul school realistically, but the two streams of artistic consciousness have blended to reveal a glimpse of something deeper than the daily routine. The art of India has always been sensitive to this duality, and it is perhaps one of her gifts to the world.

Dance and Drama

Every year on Republic Day (January 26) Delhi is invaded by a great river of gay colors, picturesque costumes, and dancing feet. One of the outstanding features of the annual celebration of this national holiday is the parade, which is beautifully staged on the great boulevards of New Delhi leading up to the Parliament buildings and the President's House.

First come the defense services with their precision of movement and smart appearance. But following closely after them is a procession which is probably unknown in any other great capital of the world. It comprises a large number of bands of village people in their distinctive costumes who have gathered from all over India to perform the dances which are characteristic of their own parts of the country. Men and women, whole families, come to the capital and camp there for some days, taking their turn in presenting their programs. Sometimes when they are not required to be at the stadium little bands of the dancers may be seen walking through the smart and sophisticated shopping area of New Delhi and looking at everything with bright-eyed, ingenuous curiosity. The ultramodern people who shop there,

Manipuri dance pose

Folk dance in honor of Republic Day, January 26

from foreign embassies, Indian states, and other lands, are just as intriguing to the dancers as the dancers are to the sophisticates.

To watch the performances of these visitors to the capital is a happy introduction to one of India's oldest and most important arts.

Folk Dances

The folk dances of India have some characteristics which are found in other parts of the world, for dances, like stories and proverbs, have a way of traveling great distances. Ancient dances are linked with early rock paintings, with magic and religion, especially in the form of dance-induced ecstasy.

Most common perhaps are the dances which are related to primitive agriculture. To enjoy them one must temporarily forget the mechanization of agriculture and industry which is gradually taking place in developing countries. The dances represent the basic rhythms of life on the soil—preparing the fields, sowing seed, cultivating and reaping, followed by threshing, winnowing, and grinding the grain. Just as little children often dance spontaneously either to relieve their pent-up feelings or to express their harmony with the rhythm of life around them, so may unsophisticated man be moved.

"The inner life bubbles up in his soul. The deeper rhythms move his feet to dance even as the magic of rhythm moves little children to dance. Thus if the gods give the blessings of plenty as the reward for work, man offers his gratitude through the one act which is nearest to prayer—the dance."

Dushera Festival, a folk drama that ends in a bonfire that burns demons in effigy

The many folk dances of India have been grouped under three heads:

"1. Community folk dances held on the main religious festivals and social occasions.
2. Folk dances which have been preserved by families as hereditary treasures, and by troupes who perform at birth, betrothal and marriage festivities in the village.
3. Tribal dances, rooted in aboriginal cults and expressive of their magical philosophies of life."

The dances are performed by groups of men or groups of women and occasionally by men and women together.

There is apparently some relation between the dances and what is known as men's work or as women's work. In agriculture the first tool was probably a sharpened stick, the point of which was tempered by being thrust alternately into fire and cold water. This was succeeded by the mattock or hoe, and both the implements were much used by women. When the plow was invented, plowing became man's work. There is a difference of opinion about sowing seed, as in some places it is done by women and in other districts by men. Weeding and cultivation and the cutting of grain are very largely women's work, for, as one farmer expressed it, "God made women to bend; they bend much better than men do." The removal of the sheaves of grain and the winnowing are often carried on by men; grinding the grain into flour is definitely women's work. All these occupations are reflected in the dances and songs which repeat the rhythms of agriculture. Those occupations which are chiefly women's usually have dances which are performed by women, and vice versa.

The most important musical instruments which accompany the dance are drums in great variety. Dances may, however, be accompanied by an oboe-like wind instrument and sometimes by a primitive type of stringed instrument, and of course most often by singing and clapping.

Classical dancer in a pose reminiscent of ancient sculpture

The element of magic has been mentioned in connection with agriculture-based dances. Leaping into the air is not simply an overflow of high spirits, it is thought to encourage the growth of the crops—the higher the better! Such dancing gives a tremendous sense of release from the strain of long days of toil. More than that, it is believed to encourage the fertility of crops and cattle, which of course make up the wealth of the villager.

Dancing and Machines

The distinguished modern dancer and choreographer, Uday Shankar, also known in the West, created an impressive ballet showing the place of dancing in an industrial society. The ballet is performed in three parts. In the first act we see a village full of spontaneous rhythm,

The hand pose or mudra is important in classical dancing

where it is as natural for the people to express their feelings by the dance as by breathing. Into this village comes a man who proclaims "Progress" and who succeeds in persuading the people to develop industries. In the second act we see the results of the new policy. Either by sheer force of habit or by an inward urge which had not been extinguished, the villagers attempt to dance as they did before, but something has very definitely gone wrong. Their movements resemble those of the machinery with which they have been working; rods and pistons are suggested rather than the smooth flow of muscle. The villagers become miserable. In the third act the village is visited by a community worker who has a sense of proportion, and he is able to convince the people that machinery is their servant and not their master. With the joyful sense of freedom that returns to them, the villagers once more begin to dance with their old joyous spontaneity.

Classical Dances

The other major division of Indian dances are those generally known as the temple, or classical, dances. They too are of great antiquity. There are four main schools.

The oldest is known as the *Bharat Natyam,* which has survived nearly three thousand years. Its classical exponent was the sage Bharata, who wrote his treatise on dancing in the fourth century B.C., but his work was to systematize a choreography that already existed. Bharat Natyam originated in temple rituals and until recent times was closely associated with temple services, much as early drama in England was performed in the churches or churchyards. Indeed the Sanskrit words for drama and dancing come from the same root. Unlike the development of drama in England, however, where the participants were drawn from the men and women of the parish, the early dancers of Bharat Natyam were young girls who were attendants in the temple. Eventually this was frowned upon, and the performances of the Natyam are now secularized, though the inspiration of the dance is strongly religious. It is still danced largely by women, though not by temple devotees. The Natyam expresses the yearning of the soul

for the divine by a most complicated series of gestures and footwork. Its home is in south India, though it is also well-known in other parts of the country. It was carried to the countries of Southeast Asia, such as Java, Cambodia, and Siam, where it may still be seen in various adaptations.

Kathakali is a more masculine type of dancing and takes its themes from the Hindu epics, the *Ramayana* and the *Mahabharata*. It was developed in the seventeenth century and perhaps represents a hybrid between the folk dances of Kerala and the Sanskrit dance drama. It employs gorgeous and sometimes startling masks and make-up combined with amazing headgear and archaic costumes.

Kathak is essentially a north Indian dance and is largely based on the sports and amours of Krishna. Many episodes of daily life are brought into the plot.

186

Manipuri which developed in Assam is also based on the Krishna cycle but is more suggestive of its folk origin than is Kathak.

The Krishna of the dances is one of the most popular of Hindu deities. He is the legendary cowherd of Brindaban who combined very human qualities with magical powers. The influence of the Krishna cycle in folk dancing, music, art, and drama has been enormous.

These schools of dancing are now becoming familiar to people not only in various parts of India but also in the West, partly from the visits of tourists to India, and partly by the tours of Indian troupes in Western countries.

In these classical dances all parts of the body come into play; the dance becomes mime, and the mime develops into ballet or drama almost imperceptibly. The influence of the older traditions is apparent in modern Indian films which make fuller use of dancing and singing than the average Western film. It must be admitted that Indian drama is being hard pressed by the film, but good dancing still gets a warm response. Perhaps the future of the dance and drama is linked with the faith of the nation. Both are considered religious in inspiration and are usually begun with an act of worship.

Jewelry

It is an easy transition to pass from dance and drama to a consideration of jewelry, especially that worn by women, because it has for many centuries been an important part of dress in India for both sexes but perhaps especially for women. If one looks at the sculptures of Ellora or the paintings of Ajanta, it will soon be seen that the garments of the period were scanty and diaphanous, and the higher the status of the person portrayed, the more the costume seemed to be composed of jewelry of many kinds. In fact, as someone once remarked, "In Ajanta only the servants wear clothes!"

Jewelry may be important to a woman for economic reasons. Formerly a woman had few personal rights, but she did have the privilege of owning jewelry which could not be taken from her by her husband's creditors.

Jewelry was often an award for valued services. A former princely state instituted an order of the golden anklet, and a man who received this honor was entitled to wear the anklet at court functions. (Ordinarily golden ornaments are never worn on the feet.)

Moreover, the patterns of jewelry indicate the part of the country from which the wearer comes, her social status, the economic resources of the family, and the artistic traditions of her environment.

The designs of jewelry still tend to be conventional, though modern ideas and fashion are having an influence. Traditionally, however, the landlord's wife and the peasant women may wear ornaments of different metals and widely different monetary value, but the basic design may be similar. In one case the ornament will be made of gold or silver, in the other of an alloy known as white metal or of brass. In all cases baser metals are used for the ornaments of the feet, such as anklets and toe rings. Earrings may be of gold set with jewels or of silver.

The list of varieties of jewelry or ornaments is a long one. We may include amulets or charms, which are often worn (the *tawiz*). They may not strictly be classified as ornaments even though the workmanship is often very fine.

Peasant women tend to wear a good deal of jewelry, and of them it may truly be said that

"With rings on her fingers and bells on her toes
She shall make music wherever she goes."

Ornaments are worn on the forehead. Earrings are of many designs and may be attached to any part of the ear, not merely the lobe; they are worn by men as well as women. The nose is decorated with either a pendant ring or a stud in one nostril. Around the neck are many varieties of necklaces, either chains or large flat collars. Most important is the wedding necklace. The arms are decorated with bangles and bracelets both above and below the elbow. Legs are similarly laden with anklets, so that it becomes quite impossible for a woman so decorated to move around quietly. An Indian poet says that the sound is like "the chattering of swans beside the red lotus." Rings of course are worn on

188

both toes and fingers, and tiny bells may be attached to them. The waists and hips are encircled by gold and silver chains or belts, but this is a mark of affluence.

Nowadays much less jewelry is worn, but on the occasion of a family wedding or special event there is a blaze of gold and gems. India has been the source of many gems in the past, and some of the traditional collections are quite remarkable.

Textiles

The textiles of India have been famous for centuries and have found their way to many parts of the world. The subject is too vast for more than a brief introduction to it. It includes weaving, embroidery, painting and printing on fabrics, using the "tie and dye" method of obtaining interesting variations in pattern and texture, and many other skills.

Weaving is an extremely ancient skill in India. The study of a fragment of dyed cloth found in an Egyptian tomb which dates back to the eighth century A.D. has led to the belief that it originated in Gujerat in western India.

Early travelers in India mentioned the fabrics they saw there. For example, Megasthenes the Greek spoke of the gorgeous gold and colored embroidered court costumes. Bernier wrote of the colorful painted cloths which lined the tents in camp—still a characteristic of Indian tents of any description.

The love of gay color seems sometimes to be related to the landscape. Those who live in the desert regions stretching from Sindh to Rajputana relieve the monotony of the scenery by the strong brilliant colors which the women habitually wear.

Early designs on cloth were similar to designs on pottery. Even now the patterns on women's clothes in some places can be traced back to the painted pottery of Harappa and other centers of the Indus Valley civilization. The designs are primarily geometric, but quite early there was a development of floral patterns and other designs taken from nature.

The export of Indian printed cottons began early and was extensive from Sindh to Babylon five thousand years ago. From the early days of this present era Indian textiles were carried to Egypt, Arabia, Turkestan, China, Siam, and Java.

Whole villages were involved in the production of these fabrics which were so extensively used both at home and abroad. When Europeans discovered the calicos and muslins, they were taken up with enthusiasm and were popular from the fifteenth century for two hundred years or more. They had a good deal of influence on English design, and the chintzes which are typical of English furnishing originated in India, including the name of the material. With the Industrial Revolution and the desire to capture such a lucrative trade for the home market, machines began to make materials that took the place of the handsome fabrics, and the Indian market was hard hit. The discovery of synthetic dyes which were used instead of the native-grown madder and indigo added to the hardship and suffering of villagers in India.

In time, however, India learned to make her own mill cloth and export it to Africa and Asia. A new national pride revived interest in Indian cloth, and a country-wide organization of spinners and weavers and the development of marketing agencies are bringing new vitality to the industry. It stands to reason that there can be no real competition between handloom and mill cloth, but there is a place for both of them in the Indian economy.

A fresh impetus was given to the idea of buying home products by the fact that it was linked with the national movement and known as *Swadeshi.* The homespun and woven cloth known as *khadder* which was worn by Gandhi and other national leaders became the insignia of the Congress Party. The present interest in handloom fabrics, however, includes materials of fine quality, and all the artistic skills of the past are linked with a modern youthful note.

The Craftsmen

It has been impossible in this chapter to include even a bare list of the variety of Indian arts and crafts in many materials and forms. But we must not forget the men and women who have kept the beauty of color and form from being forgotten through the centuries. In the words of an Indian writer:

"The miracle that faces us in studying the history of civilization is that always at least a few men have risen to the occasion. And, surprisingly, they were not often monarchs but the humble folk, the artisans, who rescued from the depths of the dark the glow of knowledge and brought an extraordinary skill to the making of objects, which exalts man above the state of savagery, refines his instincts, and leaves him the legacy of an inherited culture, with which to defy the more destructive aspects of nature and the rapacity of other, less sensitive men.

"And in Kashmir, in spite of the most dire political oppression for hundreds of years, the miracle of the job well done emerges again and again right until our own times.

"Few parts of our country can show a more continuous tradition of arts and crafts than this valley, where one oppressive feudal conqueror followed the previous feudal lord, but where the little men, often weak and easily subdued, succeeded in civilizing their conquerors for centuries. Ethnically a mixed stock, they seem early to have acquired a peculiar sensitiveness to the nuances of the heavenly landscape where they came to live. And from [this environment] they took [their] motifs, and from their struggle to live they evolved with their deft hands the living tradition of handicrafts, which has made the word 'Cashmere' . . . a synonym of a quality of workmanship, the legend of which will survive even if all the most precious shawls in the museums of the world should be destroyed."

Indira Nehru Gandhi, first woman to be elected head of a major national government

What of today? Are there any springs still
functioning from which we can refresh and
strengthen ourselves?

—NEHRU

India's Role in the World

The evening in Bombay was lovely and especially so on the seashore
at Chowpatty Sands. There Ted and Jim went for their last evening
in India after a gay restaurant party at which some of their friends
played host. Surjit had come to town for the occasion bringing greetings
from many people "up-country." Ahmed came from Delhi and brought
messages from people there. There were also the journalist, Sivaram,
and his wife, Kamala. As the little party settled down on the sands,
the boys thought they had never seen a more beautiful city. From
Malabar Hill on the right they had looked down on the curving Marine
Drive which sparkled with lights and is often called the Queen's Necklace. Behind them were the dignified buildings of a university college.
And in front of them, in the moonlight, lay the expanse of the Indian
Ocean. The freighters and the fishing boats moving slowly over the
ocean reminded the boys of their departure the next day.

"How delightful it all is! India is a very beautiful country," sighed
Jim.

"Speaking of ships, or looking at ships, how do you feel about leaving?" asked Sivaram.

"Much sadder than I expected," said Jim. "Of course, I'll be glad
to see my home and friends again, but I shall often think of India and
my friends here, and I hope to return someday."

"Me, too," said Ted.

"I am glad that we are leaving from Bombay and will be arriving in New York," said Jim. "The two cities remind me of one another, at least Bombay reminds me of New York, and I hope it will be the other way round too."

"Why?" asked Kamala, somewhat surprised.

"Well, both are island cities and both have tall buildings and crowded streets."

"Yes, Bombay has some pretty high buildings though nothing like New York. When Bombay needed more land it was reclaimed from the sea."

In astonishment Jim said, "Where? Not that lovely Marine Drive?"

"Oh, yes," said Sivaram, "that was under the sea a few years ago. Isn't it a magnificent achievement?"

"But aside from being an island, and crowded, there is an energy and liveliness about both Bombay and New York that make them good places to visit. Both are great ports and very cosmopolitan."

"What sort of questions are your people at home going to ask you?" said Kamala. "Come, tell us, and maybe we can help you get your answers ready."

"The first question many people will ask us," said Ted, "is 'What is India like?' What would you say?"

The Indians agreed that that was a hard one. India is so many things to so many people.

"Of course it is an impossible question," said Jim, "though a natural one. Just the other day I heard of a Canadian girl who wanted to see India, and she said, 'If I could just visit India for half an hour—!' If it were in my power, I would certainly have granted her wish. As long as visitors don't think they know all about India after a short visit, it is a good thing for them to have at least one mental picture of what India looked like to them."

Pictures of India

"But what will *you* remember about India?" Sivaram asked Jim.

"Let's begin with what India looks like, just as we begin with what a person looks like. I shall never forget the grandeur of the snow peaks

194

Marine Drive along the waterfront of Bombay

in the north, or the gentle Blue Mountains of the south. I shall think of the dense jungle I saw in some areas and the open parkland too. But always I shall think of the rivers. Where else can a river be adored as a goddess and then harnessed and made to work? The rivers themselves are either majestic and constant in their flow or teasing and capricious, until each river seems to have a personality of its own."

"What are you going to tell your friends about the people—about us?" asked Kamala with a teasing look. "India isn't all mountains and rivers and Queen's Necklaces, you know."

"You've seen the mills," said Surjit.

"And the villages," said Chandra, who had come all the way from Gopalpur. "What are you going to say, and can you make people understand?"

The boys, Ted and Jim, looked at each other.

Then Ted laughed, "Don't you know that is why we are sailing instead of flying? We hope it will give us time to sort things out in our minds. But you can help by asking questions now. So just keep on."

"Is there anything in your visit to India which you feel is incomplete, anything you wish had been different?" asked Ahmed.

"Yes," said Jim, "one thing I regret very much is that we did not come in time to see Pandit Nehru while he was Prime Minister of India. Often I have had the feeling that he must have been a great personality because his influence is still so strongly felt."

Ted nodded agreement, and the conversation about Nehru became general.

Homage to Nehru

"Since he has left such a marked impression on the country, we hope that he will be more than a legend. We hope that his principles of peace, justice, and freedom for people everywhere will be cherished."

"It seems to me remarkable that he endeared himself particularly to simple folk though he was not a simple man. You know his birthday was celebrated as National Children's Day, and special anniversary stamps were issued. Panditji made friends with children easily, and he was known by them as 'Uncle Nehru.' "

"Many people who met him did not realize that they were in the presence of a distinguished statesman and scholar. Oh, they knew that there was greatness in him, but after all, he belonged to them and was their friend. He went to school and college in England, you know, and always spoke in a soft, clear, English accent. He really did not know Hindi until he went into politics—no more did Gandhi—but both men learned to use Hindi effectively and spoke with a simplicity and directness that was most pleasing to listen to."

"It was Nehru who led India into the councils of the world and took his place with dignity and respect among the representatives of

Mr. Nehru explaining the Beating the Retreat Ceremony to Queen Elizabeth during a Royal Tour

the Commonwealth. It was not surprising that his sister, Madame Pandit, also became famous abroad and served as Chairman of the United Nations' General Assembly."

Prime Minister Shastri (1964–1966)

"But what are we to say about Nehru's successor, Lal Bahadur Shastri?" asked Ted. "He was so little known in the West that we are certain to be asked about him."

"He was a man of courage and serenity," said Chandra. "He had the integrity that comes through years of self-discipline. His strong leadership lay in his teamwork; he knew the art of 'consensus' better than most people."

"The sudden news of Shastri's death immediately after he had signed a peace pact with Pakistan shocked millions of people in India and abroad, just as President Kennedy's death profoundly grieved the people of the world," said Ted. "I think you will be interested in a news clipping I just received from home about a memorial service to Shastri in Toronto. Dr. R. C. Gupta said: 'Shastri's action in signing the Declaration of Tashkent marked him as a great Prime Minister, just as President Kennedy's action on Cuba marked him as a great President. Each gave within his short tenure of office the indisputable proof of his greatness. I wonder to what height they would have gone, had they been spared another five years.' "

Women Lead in Service

"The appointment of Mrs. Indira Gandhi as Prime Minister shortly after Shastri's death was a thrilling achievement for the people of India and a challenge to the women of the world," said Jim.

"Yes" Kamala agreed. "Mrs. Gandhi is not related to Mahatma Gandhi, but she is Nehru's only child. Like her father, she has a broad education—school in Switzerland and university training in India and at Oxford."

"Mrs. Gandhi brings to her high office dignity and ability, combined with a world view gained by much travel and wide interests," added

198

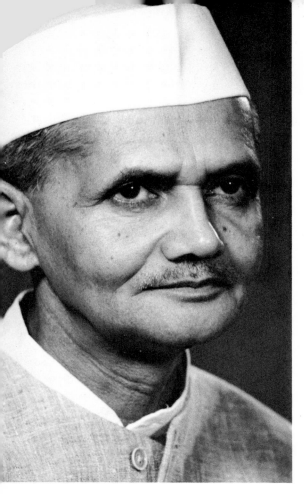

Chandra. "The Indian people have shown wisdom in selecting a person with such marked ability, though it is unprecedented to choose a woman as head of the government, and she has shown courage in accepting the leadership of her country at such a difficult time in its history."

"It is rather interesting," said Kamala, "that ever since independence the Ministers of Health in the central government have been women. And how those women have worked! Delhi can't contain them, but they go out and see things for themselves."

"My mother is going to be very much interested when I tell her what Indian women are doing for the reconstruction of the country," said Ted. "The other day we saw two girl students, about our age, who were spending hours every week teaching women to read under the most uncomfortable conditions. I thought those girls showed the most marvelous patience and cheerfulness, and they were certainly getting results."

"And aren't the women happy with their achievement?" said Surjit. "Do you know that a group of working women in my area kept on studying after they had learned to read? They have reached grade five and are still going strong!"

"What gave the women of India these new ideas?"

"Three things, I think," said Kamala. "The first, of course, was education. At one time many people believed that it was not possible to educate a girl; others said it might be possible, but would certainly be dangerous!"

"Teaching a woman to read is like putting a knife in the hand of a monkey," quoted Sivaram with a smile.

"But the time came when girls did learn to read and become educated," continued Kamala. "Their first teachers were dedicated women, many of them from the West.

The new Indian family can expect a longer and better life

"The next factor was the call of Gandhi for women to take an active part in the movement for independence. Gandhi had a high opinion of what women could do, and they realized it. Once a woman had left her pots and pans, however, and taken part in a procession or gone to jail as a political prisoner, she was never the same again. She had become aware of the world outside her home.

"The third factor was the rise of many women's organizations. The All-India Women's Conference was one of them. It works for the educational and social advancement of women, and the results have been remarkable. You know that India has more women in public life than has any other country, and a large proportion of those women were trained by their experience with the A.I.W.C."

India's Basic Democracy

"I think it is a wonderful thing," said Jim, "to see democracy at work in the second largest nation of the world. True, it isn't always like the democracy in which I grew up, but the basic principles are the same: justice, equality, liberty, fraternity. I know that the government of India is responsive to the will of the people; and I have been told that the general elections in India involve more voters than in any other country. India is so very old culturally, and yet quite young as a democratic nation."

Surjit grinned, "It is something like the contrast in our family: in all sorts of knowledge about modern life, planes, spacecraft, electronics, and so on, I am much older than my father, but when it comes to many other things, the old man knows better than I do. I have the greatest respect for the shrewdness and good judgment of the Indian farmer like my father, but we young people are interested in change and progress, and we are in a hurry."

Sivaram reported, "India as a whole has made good progress. While the population has increased more than 20 per cent in ten years, industrial production went up 75 per cent, agricultural production increased by 45 per cent. The new emphasis on education has raised the number of people who can read and write from 8 per cent to 30 per cent

—four times as many as before. People are living longer; the average life expectancy has risen from 34 to 46."

A Stamp Tells a Story

"Speaking of public life and knowing of your interest in stamps," said Chandra to Ted, "I have brought one for your collection." Chandra produced it from his pocket, and at the same time he brought out a small flashlight, as the evening was now too dark for stamp viewing.

The stamp they were examining was one of an issue of 1962 commemorating a law setting up village councils (*Panchayati Raj*) as the acknowledged form of local self-government for rural areas. The word "panch," meaning "five," refers to the traditional committee of five members. The new type of village council, however, consists of members elected from among themselves by all the people of the village. In quite a remarkable way the stamp is a miniature of the government of the new India.

In the background of the stamp is outlined a map of India. In the lower half is a village council holding a meeting under a banyan tree. The group includes half-a-dozen men and two women. It is interesting that the women are not sitting by themselves to one side in the traditional manner, but beside the men, and with uncovered heads, obviously enjoying a sense of equality. They are present not as women but as citizens.

In the upper portion of the stamp is the House of the People, the *Lok Sabha* (Parliament) in New Delhi.

"There on one small, pink postage stamp we have the pictorial representation of Indian democracy today," said Sivaram with quiet satisfaction.

"But is there nothing between the village council and Parliament?" asked Jim.

"Yes," said Surjit, "the state legislatures with elected members. At the head of the Republic of India is the President, Sir Radhakrishnan. He is a philosopher, you know. I once saw a book about ancient Greece which was called, 'When Philosophers Were Kings.' Don't you think we have something like that today? Of course the government is not in his hands but is carried on by the Prime Minister and the Cabinet who are responsible to Parliament. It is patterned after the British system."

Indian stamp commemorating the law recognizing village councils as local governments

Cricket

Ahmed said, "That reminds me—not long ago an eminent Indian said that he felt his country should be grateful for three gifts the British had brought: a constitutional government, the English language which is now international, and the game of cricket."

"Cricket?" said the boys together. "Cricket!" Their friends laughed at their astonishment.

"Cricket is very popular in India, you know, and it is not only a game, it is an outlook on life, a pattern of behavior. If you hear an action alluded to as 'not cricket,' you know that it just 'isn't done.' I think myself that it is a fine thing to have young India growing up with a respect for teamwork, a sporting spirit, and a sense of fair play."

"You see little boys all over the country playing their version of cricket on a vacant patch of land with homemade or improvised equipment."

Girl throwing a cricket ball on Sports Day at a college

A Hindu bride and groom in wedding finery

What Are the Youth Like?

"Now for a difficult question," said Surjit, "but don't shirk it. When you go home many of your friends are going to say, 'What are the young people of India like?'"

"That's not so difficult after all," said Jim. "We think you are grand. Of course you have your difficulties, but so have we."

"What are some of ours?" asked Surjit.

"Well, the gulf between the generations is wider here, in many cases. The other day a girl was telling me how very hard it was to live as an educated person when her mother was illiterate. I can see that a girl in that situation may have a really hard time in expressing her point of view."

"One big difficulty," said Sivaram, "is that our ideas about discipline and conventions have changed. Juvenile delinquency is not as serious in India as in some countries, I believe, but I heard a police officer

Students at a modern school

say that the most difficult young people were the students, who may even strike against their university. This is so contrary to all Indian traditions that it is startling."

"On the other hand," said Kamala, "there is a great deal of interest among students in social problems. They may debate points for endless hours, but if they are given an opportunity, they really do get out and do some useful work. I have seen students digging alongside villagers to make a new road or a well. They like to see practical achievements."

Communism

"Americans are sure to ask about Communism in India," said Jim.

Ahmed replied, "It has been very well said that Communism thrives where there is ignorance, apathy, and the lack of a social conscience. This is not the situation in India today. The war on ignorance is steadily going forward on all fronts. There is still too much apathy, but it is not characteristic of youth. And between the women and youth a strong social conscience is developing."

"But there is so much to be done," said Jim. "Look at the problems if you can bear to do it—illiteracy, poverty, and disease."

"Yes, I know," said Ahmed. "Don't think we don't see these things. We do. But let me tell you this: we are the first generation really to be aware of these facts as problems. And we are not 'sweeping them under the rug'—to use an expression I learned from you the other day. We are facing the population problem and doing something about it. We are spending vast sums of public money on education. Five times as many students are in high school as in 1847. Now don't shake your head and say, 'Too little, too late.' It is much, much more

A festival on the Ganges River at Hardwar

than has ever been done before, and it will grow with its own momentum."

Over-population

"Another thing I know they are going to ask is about the 'population explosion.' They will say, 'Isn't anything being done about that?'"
"Is there enough food? Can India grow more?"
"Is caste as strong as ever?"
"Is India a really democratic country?"
"Is India interested in the atom bomb?"
"What is India's present leadership like?"
"Stop! Stop!" said Ahmed. "What mouthfuls!" and they all laughed.
"About population, we can tell them that people are really working at family planning on the one hand, and on the production of more food on the other."
One of the boys pointed out to sea. "Beneath those waters lie great unused food supplies, and Canada and Norway are working with India to develop them. It is the same story in many versions. Friendly nations give their aid in various ways, and India always does as much or more to meet it."

Afro-Asian Links

"India is now one of the world powers, and we must realize that. What about India's role in Asia and Africa?" said Ted. "What shall we say about it?"
"Let's talk about Africa first," said Ahmed. "It is true that the average Indian does not have much awareness of Africa, especially of the new African nations. But the situation is changing rapidly. While we have not been fully aware of the new African nations, they have been keenly aware of us. In our time the achievement of independent nationhood by India has not only influenced other Asian countries but Africa too. Many of the new African states have been encouraged and excited by the way India has achieved independence and leadership in world affairs."

Three Indians Who Spoke for Africa

Ahmed then went on to tell them about the three great Indians who spoke for the cause of Africa in this century.

The first was Gandhi. In South Africa he worked out his techniques for nonviolent protests. True, the condition of his fellow countrymen was his chief concern, but he maintained his interest in the African struggle even after he returned to India. Now Gandhi's principles are influencing the civil rights movement for Negroes in America.

The next great Indian carried things further. V. S. Srinivasa Shastri (no relation to the Prime Minister) was a great orator—"Shastri of the golden tongue," he was called. Shastri visited Kenya on behalf of the Indian settlers there and also represented their case in Britain. He became convinced that the Indian problem was subordinate to the position of Africans in their own country and encouraged Indians in Africa to look at the larger issues of "African paramountcy."

The third step was taken by Jawaharlal Nehru, who urged the importance of Afro-Asian solidarity in international affairs. It was through Nehru that the government of India began offering scholarships to African students who wished to study in India, and about six hundred of them are now taking advantage of the opportunity. India has also sent a number of experts in education and technology to Africa. It remains to be seen how the present energetic policy of China to win the new African nations will affect the situation.

We must not forget the influence of trade, and that for a long time India and East Africa have traded with one another. Trade has now been further extended, as for example, India buys cotton from the U.A.R. and sells them tea and jute in return. The present value of Indo-African trade is about $240,000,000.

In regard to Indian relations with the other countries of Asia, the picture is a changing one.

"As I heard it said in Delhi," remarked Ahmed, "it is the realities of trade, aid, and information that are likely to count most in the relations of the future of one country with another, as the Asian and African countries move toward more substantial economic development in a world concerned with the politics of power."

"It is generally admitted that India has a unique role to play in Asia," said Sivaram. "Lord Wavell, when he was Viceroy of India, expressed it well when he referred to India as the 'Shield for Peace in Asia.' "

"Is that because of the shape of the country?" asked Jim.

"Partly, I suppose, and partly because of Lord Wavell's sensitive perception—he was a great lover of poetry, you know. India has consistently stood for peaceful negotiations among nations, and peace with honor," said Sivaram solemnly. "Let us hope that she succeeds."

Good-bye

"Jim, what are you thinking about?" asked Ahmed. "You have been quiet for quite a few minutes."

"I'm thinking about *water*," said Jim with considerable feeling. "I shall not feel the same about water again. I hope that never again shall I be as thirsty as I have been sometimes in India! All the rest of my life I shall rush to turn off a leaky tap. And I shall startle my mother by looking at the first glass of water she gives me and asking suspiciously, 'Has this water been boiled?' " Then he changed his tone and added somewhat shyly, "I shall think it wonderful that I can take water from the hand of anyone, and that anyone can take water from mine."

The others laughed and a little silence fell on the group. Then Ted turned to Ahmed and said, "I guess we'll have to stop talking at last, but I don't want to leave India without hearing you sing once more. I should especially appreciate hearing that song of Tagore that students like so much."

So Ahmed sang:

> Where the mind is without fear
>   and the head is held high;
> Where knowledge is free;
> Where the world has not been broken up
>   into fragments by narrow domestic walls;

210

Where words come out from the depths of truth;
Where tireless striving stretches
   its arms towards perfection;
Where the clear stream of reason has not lost its way
   into the dreary desert sand of dead habit;
Where the mind is led forward by thee
   into ever-widening thought and action—
Into that heaven of freedom, my Father,
   let my country awake.

A Reading List

CLASSICS AND CLASSICS RETOLD

The Geeta: The Gospel of the Lord Shri Krishna, translated from the original Sanskrit by Shri Purohitswami. London: Faber, 1959.

Gods, Demons and Others, by R. K. Narayan. London: Heinemann, 1965.

Jataka Tales: Birth Stories of the Buddha, retold by Ethel Beswick. Hollywood-by-the-Sea, Fla.: Transatlantic, 1956.

The Ramayana and the Mahabharata, condensed into English verse by Romesh C. Dutt. London: Dent, 1955. (Everyman's Library)

The Ramayana as told by Aubrey Menen. New York: Scribner, 1954. A satire of the true Ramayana.

Stories from the Indian Classics, by Vishwanath S. Naravane. New York: Asia Publishing House, 1962.

Shakuntala and Other Writings, translated with an introduction by Arthur W. Ryder.

RELIGION

Buddhism, by Henri Arvon. New York: Walker, 1962. (Paperback)

The Light of Asia, by Sir Edwin Arnold. London: Routledge, 1959. A life of Gautama Buddha in verse.

The Nature of Hinduism, by Louis Renou. New York: Walker, 1962. (Paperback)

The Wisdom of India, by Lin Yutang. New York: Random House, 1942.

SOCIAL STUDIES

Behind Mud Walls, by William and Charlotte Wiser. Berkeley: University of California Press, 1963.

Blossoms in the Dust, by Kusum Nair. London: Duckworth, 1961. A report on village community projects.

Caste in India, by J. H. Hutton. New York: Oxford, 1963.

Anguish of India, by Ronald Segal. New York: Stein & Day, 1965.

The Man Eater of Kumaon, by Jim Corbett. New York: Oxford, 1957.

The Monsoon Lands of Asia, by R. R. Rawson. Chicago: Aldine Publishing Co., 1964.

My India, by Jim Corbett. New York: Oxford, 1952.

ART AND LITERATURE

The Art of India: Tradition of Indian Sculpture, Painting and Architecture, by Stella Kranrisch. London: Phaidon, 1954.

Collected Poems and Plays, by Rabindranath Tagore. New York: Macmillan, 1955.

A History of Far Eastern Art, by Sherman E. Lee. London: Thames and Hudson, 1954.

Thirteen Tibetan Tankas, by Edna Brynner. Indian Hills, Colo.: Falcon's Wing Press, 1956. Based on Jataka Tales.

Three Plays, by Rabindranath Tagore. New York: Oxford, 1950.

BIOGRAPHY

From Fear Set Free, by Nayantara Sahgal. London: Gollancz, 1962.

A Gandhi Reader, by Homer A. Jack. New York: Grove Press, 1956.

Madame Ambassador: Vijaya Lakshmi Pandit, by Anne Guthrie. New York: Harcourt, Brace and World, 1962.

Prison and Chocolate Cake, by Nayantara Sahgal. New York: Knopf, 1954.

Remember the House, by Santha Rama Rau. New York: Harper, 1956.

Seven Summers: The Story of an Indian Childhood, by Mulk Raj Anand. London: Hutchinson, 1951.

NOVELS

The Big Heart, by Mulk Raj Anand. London: Hutchinson.

Binodini, by Rabindranath Tagore. New York: Heinman, 1959.

The Financial Expert, by R. K. Narayan. East Lansing, Mich.: Michigan State College Press, 1953.

The Guide, by R. K. Narayan. London: Methuen, 1958.

The Princes, by Manohar Malgonkar. London: Hamish Hamilton, 1963.

The Printer of Malgudi, by R. K. Narayan. East Lansing, Mich.: Michigan State University Press, 1957.

The Serpent and the Rope, by Rao Raja. New York: Pantheon, 1963.

A Time To Be Happy, by Nayantara Sahgal. London: Gollancz, 1958.

To Whom She Will, by R. Prawar Jhabvala. London: Allen and Unwin, 1955.

Highlights in Indian History

1658–1707	Aurangzeb, the last of the "Grand Moguls"
1858	Deposition of the last Mogul emperor

THE DOOR TO THE WEST OPENS

1498	Vasco da Gama lands at Calicut
1510	Affonso de Albuquerque occupies Goa for Portugal
1609	The East India Company sets up first trading post in Surat
1615–18	English embassy of Sir Thomas Roe to the Mogul Court
1640	Madras set up as an East India Company post
1660	Bombay given to Charles II of England as part of dowry of Catherine of Portugal
1690	Calcutta established by Job Charnock for East India Company
1857–58	The Sepoy Revolt or Indian Mutiny
1858	The British Crown takes over administration from the East India Company; Queen Victoria named Empress of India

SELF-DETERMINATION

1883	Organization of Indian National Congress, a major political party dedicated to "self-rule"
1947	Independent India becomes a voluntary member of the Commonwealth, August 15
1948	Death of Mohandas K. Gandhi, "Father of the Nation," (born October 2, 1869)
1949	Constitution adopted by Constituent Assembly
1950	Republic Day, January 26, Constitution comes into force
1955	State visit of Bulganin and Krushchev from Soviet Union
1959	State visit of President Eisenhower from the United States
1961	State visit of Queen Elizabeth II of England
1962–63	Chinese invasion of India
1964	Death of Prime Minister Jawaharlal Nehru (born 1889)
1966	Signing of Tashkent Peace Pact with Pakistan; sudden death of Shastri, January 11
	Indira Nehru Gandhi elected Prime Minister, January 19

Index

218

222

About the Author

L. Winifred Bryce was born in Japan, but educated in Canada. She received a doctorate in sociology at the University of Toronto.

Dr. Bryce and her husband spent forty years in India as educators and missionaries. At Indore, they set up the school of social work. Although Dr. Bryce "retired" twice, she was called back on two occasions to stabilize the administration of the school she loved so much, which found itself in difficulties under the new government regime in India.

Dr. Bryce is the author of seven books published both in English and Hindi. Her book *India at the Threshold* is well-known in America and Britain. She has also contributed countless articles to outstanding periodicals throughout the world and is internationally known as an authority on India. She is the mother of six children and has preserved the unusually rare quality of never cutting the lines of communication with associates of all age groups, sexes, and nationalities.

World Neighbors

Written to introduce teen-age Americans to their contemporaries in other lands, these books are well-documented, revealing presentations of our world neighbors. Based on firsthand knowledge of the country and illustrated with unusual photographs, the text is informal and inviting. Geographical, historical, and cultural data are woven unobtrusively into accounts of daily life. Maps, working index, chronology, and bibliography are useful additions.

ALASKA Pioneer State, *by Norma Spring*
CANADA Young Giant of the North, *by Adelaide Leitch*
CENTRAL AMERICA Lands Seeking Unity,
    by Charles Paul May
EQUATORIAL AFRICA New World of Tomorrow,
    by Glenn Kittler
GREECE & THE GREEKS, *by Lyn Harrington*
HAWAII, U.S.A., *by Lily Edelman*
INDIA Land of Rivers, *by L. Winifred Bryce*
ISRAEL New People in an Old Land, *by Lily Edelman*
JAPAN Crossroads of East and West, *by Ruth Kirk*
MEXICO Land of Hidden Treasure, *by Ellis Credle*
THE SOVIET UNION A View from Within,
    by Franklin Folsom
THE UNITED KINGDOM A New Britain, *by Marian Moore*